TIMES OF REFRESHING

Keys to Living an Empowered Life

JE'NISE J. GOSS

Times of Refreshing: *Keys to Living an Empowered Life*

Pastor Je'Nise J. Goss
Greater Deep Tabernacle of Faith
P.O. Box 2033
Apex, NC 27502
919-629-2147
www.pastorjenise.com

ISBN-10: 0970719213
ISBN-13: 978-0-9707192-1-8

Printed in the United States of America

DEDICATION

This book is dedicated to my amazing husband,
Prophet L. Donnell Goss, Sr., who stepped into my life and opened
up a world of which I never knew I could be a part. Thank you for
teaching me to dream and helping me to fly!

ACKNOWLEDGEMENTS

To my children, Ayisha, Desiree, Monique and Donnell, Jr., who
believed in my dream and helped me push forward, I love you!
May God Expand in You!

To my family, friends and ministry partners
who sowed into my vision, Thank You!
May God multiply your seed 10,000-fold!

TABLE OF CONTENTS

Preface   6

Introduction   8

Chapter One: Can't Breathe Without Him!   13

Chapter Two: Sometimes You Have To Stop and Exhale!   29

Chapter Three: Who Are You?   47

Chapter Four: You Got to Fight To Win!   63

Chapter Five: Victory Over Temptation   75

Chapter Six: You're Bigger Than That!   89

Chapter Seven: Cast Your Cares   111

Chapter Eight: MOVE!   123

Chapter Nine: Positioned To Win!   139

APPENDIX: Refreshing Thoughts and Affirmations   151

PREFACE

"If you can't fly then run, if you can't run then walk, if you can't walk then crawl. But whatever you do, you have to keep moving forward." ~**Martin Luther King Jr.**

One day I woke up and I found myself surrounded by B-R-O-K-E-N-N-E-S-S - broken pieces all around me, shattered dreams cutting the depths of my mind, broken promises piercing my heart, shattered memories cutting the very depths of my soul. Everything that I thought I had was wrapped up in the life of someone else - all of my hope, all of my joy, all of my peace, all of my praise, all of my understanding, all of my tears… and here they are all in little pieces surrounding me. No wholeness, just brokenness; no joy, just sorrow; no understanding, just confusion; no laughter, just this frown.

Swinging back and forth through my emotions, up and down, hoping to always please someone…anyone.

Looking for acceptance, looking for affirmation, looking for approval, just needing to feel that I was needed, appreciated, important, special, loved… Now, my cup was full *(at least I thought it was)*, but every time I would fill it, a part of me seemed to seep out and later I would discover that my cup was empty.

Swinging back and forth through my emotions, up and down, hoping to always please someone…anyone.

I was the flyer and I wanted anyone to be the catcher, just as long as I felt safe. I needed to understand why I always needed someone to fill a void, but I had no idea how it got there. How did that crack get there anyway?

I discovered that it began in my childhood and I never healed. My mother, my father, my teachers, I was always looking for someone to make me feel safe. When my mother failed, I swung to my father. When my father failed, I swung to my teacher. When my teacher failed, I swung to a friend. Now, at the age of... I still find myself...

Swinging back and forth through my emotions, up and down, hoping to always please someone...ANYONE!

I need to get off of this trapeze, this pendulum. My arms are tired of swinging. My hands are weak. I cannot hold on much longer. I must let go of this constant need to need someone... ANYONE! I must make my dismount! I must let go! I must let go! I must let go... but this time landing on my feet!

INTRODUCTION

"Then the Lord God formed man from the dust of the ground and breathed into his nostrils the breath or spirit of life, and man became a living being." (Genesis 2:7)

BUZZZZZZZZZZZZZ! It's 6:00 a.m. The alarm clock is blaring. You jump out of the bed, sleepwalk to the shower, get dressed, make breakfast, feed the kids, walk the dog, put some last minute touches on the presentation that is due on your boss' desk by 9:00 a.m., drop the kids at school, grab that much needed cup of hot java, sprint into your office, flop in your chair and begin the daily grind...

What thoughts run through your mind? Are you thinking about what's next on your agenda? Are you trying to figure out how you will pay your bills? Does it seem as if you have more bills than money? Are you wondering how everything will come together? Do you start to feel that panicked feeling that causes your heart to race, your feet to pace, your hands to start tapping the desk or do you just grab the middle of your forehead and squeeze? Well, let me remind you...

EXHALE...

Oftentimes, we are so busy focusing on our "to-do" lists, focusing on where we have to be next, focusing on some event that is far off into the future that we forget to stop and experience the power of the moment. We forget to breathe. We forget that worry is not part of our agenda. We forget who is really in control. We forget the all-encompassing power that resides in our ability to breathe.

The word "breathe" is defined as "to be alive; to live." Breathing is one of the most unrehearsed, unplanned and least thought about activities that we do all day, yet it is one activity that we all have in common. No matter your race, creed, color, gender or socioeconomic status, if you <u>want</u> to live, you <u>must</u> breathe! Sometimes you have to stop thinking about your day-to-day agenda and just thank God for the ability to breathe, because it is another opportunity to live and <u>live well</u>!

> *"To live is the rarest thing in the world. Most people exist, that is all."* (Oscar Wilde)

For 60 seconds walk with me through a moment of exhaling.

Close your eyes and simply focus on breathing… in…out…in…out… purposeful breaths… deliberate breaths. Do not think about anything else but this moment and you will feel God's strength in every breath. When God breathed into man's nostrils, man became a living being. Every day we need that breath from God to remind us to live, to live well and to live on purpose!

When we are able to freeze time and enjoy moments with God that is when God can speak to us. Our spirits are open and receptive to His voice. It is in those moments that we can hear His still, small voice even in the midst of the noise in our lives. Isn't it amazing how the Father's voice can quiet the clamorous noise of life around you and fill your atmosphere with a peaceful stillness, a knowing that He has your life completely under control?

EXHALE...

When you learn to exhale and breathe on purpose, breathe with purpose, breathe with the determination that you are going to not just exist in this life, but live, you will find that panic is useless. If you concentrate long enough, study life long enough, trust God and follow His voice, then you will pass the test of life and everything that the Father says is yours will manifest in your experience. If you ask the Father for help, it is a promise that He will deliver you, restore you, rescue you and protect you! The key is learning how to exhale and breathe with purpose.

Now... release the hurt, release the struggle, release the pain, release the unforgiveness, release the doubt, release the fear. It's time to be refreshed. It's time to listen to the refreshing word of God that will allow you to have a new perspective on life. Your soul is longing to be refreshed with the truth that whatever is happening in your natural experience that does not line up with God's plan for your life is not the truth of you.

Do not allow your outward circumstances to dictate your level of inner peace, joy and excitement. Do not allow worry to overshadow your GOD-expectation. Focus on the goodness of God and how awesome He is, regardless of what is happening in your natural experience, for in the Spirit realm all things are working together for your good. If God said it, then He is going to perform it... regardless of what it may look like in your present circumstance. Get ready! It is time to be refreshed!

"For as many as are the promises of God, they all find their Yes [answer] in Him [Christ]. For this reason we also utter the Amen (so be it) to God through Him [in His Person and by His agency] to the glory of God." (1 Corinthians 1:20)

EXHALE...

Chapter One
CAN'T BREATHE WITHOUT HIM!

"When I consider thy heavens, the work of thy fingers, the moon and the stars, which thou hast ordained; What is man, that thou art mindful of him? and the son of man, that thou visitest him? For thou hast made him a little lower than the angels, and hast crowned him with glory and honour. Thou madest him to have dominion over the works of thy hands; thou hast put all things under his feet. (Psalm 8:3-6)

Imagine

- Have you ever stopped to imagine how much favor and power God has given you?
- Have you ever stopped to consider how much the Father has entrusted in you to deposit in the Earth?
- Have you ever stopped to ponder just how special you are to God?

Susan was a very easy-going person by nature. She loved to read, write, dance and watch old movies. Susan was very creative and had a vivid imagination. Many people liked her because of her creative abilities and her ability to make something out of nothing.

All of her life Susan found herself on center stage either in plays, public speaking or singing. Because of her appeal and her easygoing nature, Susan constantly found herself surrounded by people who wanted to be in her company. However, Susan began to notice that although many people were attracted to her gift, many were not sincere in their desire for a real relationship with her. Susan had a difficult time discerning between the two.

As a result, Susan was open to interact with anyone. She found that many people did not respect the person (Susan); they were just attracted to the gift. On her journey, Susan met many who she thought were friends, but who she later realized respected her talent more than the friendship. Over the years, Susan became discouraged. She began to distrust people, and over time she began to lose respect for herself. She became very bitter and discouraged and found herself retreating to the background in many areas of her life.

REFRESHING KEY #1
When you immerse yourself in God-reality, everything works for your good!

- Susan forgot that God created her to be great.
- Susan forgot that God gave her dominion over <u>everything</u> in the earth and that she has the power to command what she wants.
- Susan forgot her divine nature and began to succumb to the thoughts and opinions of others.

One day, Susan woke up and was disappointed that she had allowed people to cause her to disrespect the greatness that God placed within her, something which she loved so dearly. Susan wanted to get back to that place in her mind where she once dwelled.

Many people are just like Susan. Genuine greatness rests within them, but they spend so much valuable time trying to live up to the expectations of others that they lose themselves in the process. They spend so much valuable time trying to "fit into the crowd" that they forget who God created them to be, and as a result retreat into the background of their own mind, place their true, divine self on the shelf and become mediocre, or, at best, average. The truth is God breathed His breath of life on the inside of each and every one of us, but it is up to you to decide if you are going to live by the breath of God or the breath of man.

Why settle for less if God has destined you to have more? Why retreat into the background when God has destined you to be on center stage? Many people are duped into believing that man holds the key to their success, greatness, advancement and power. But the truth of the matter is - God is the Source. He will use people to open doors, but the real door-opener is Him.

The Bible says that if we seek His kingdom first, all of the other things that we seek after will be added unto us. (Matthew 6:33) You must seek Him first. What do I mean by seeking Him? You must seek God's plan and His purpose for your life. Do not allow your true self to be overshadowed by the selfish plans of others. Make sure that whatever you do, no matter what it is, aligns with God's plan and purpose for your life.

"...What I'm trying to do here is to get you to relax, to not be so preoccupied with getting, so you can respond to God's giving. People who don't know God and the way he works fuss over these things, but you know both God and how he works. Steep your life in God-reality, God-initiative, God-provisions. Don't worry about

missing out. You'll find all your everyday human concerns will be met." (Matthew 6:30-33, Message Bible)

Susan stepped back into her passion and was realigned with her purpose. Today, she is writing, singing and speaking, doing what she loves, loving what she does, fulfilling God's plan and purpose for her life and blessing the lives of others as a result.

When you immerse yourself in God-reality and God-initiative and put your faith in God's provision, everything else around you will align with the truth that God has for your life. Your family will be blessed, your finances will be blessed, your household will be blessed and the lives of those that the Father has earmarked for you to bless will be blessed. Living by His breath is paramount to your success, well-being and wholeness in this life.

"It takes more than bread to stay alive. It takes a steady stream of words from God's mouth." (Matthew 4:4, Message Bible)

Don't Relinquish the Controls!

It is very comforting to know that no matter what is happening in your natural experience, God is in control. As you commit to change your life you will begin to shift onto your path to purpose and destiny, knowing that God has everything in control. Regardless of what you are going through, regardless of what you may be facing, regardless of what your day was like even today, God is in control. As you pray to your Heavenly Father to reveal to you His plan for your life, to unveil the greatness that He breathed inside of you and to unscramble the pieces of your dream that continually filter through your mind, God responds.

Sometimes it may seem like a pipe dream. You may even question if all of these things can be true. But we serve a loving God, a God who answers our prayers, a God who understands our needs, a God who knows exactly what is best for us and a God who is true to every word that He speaks. The Father is working His divine, ultimate and timely plan behind the scenes of your everyday experience.

It is impossible to breathe without Him, the "Him" being God, the Creator, the Maker, the one who causes everything to come to pass in and through our lives. To know what God is doing in your life and to be aware of His omnipotent presence in the very core of your existence is priceless. That "knowing" empowers you to navigate life with a sense of hope, perseverance, excitement and surety. Once your confidence is restored within your being you are free to discover God in a greater, stronger and mightier way.

As I was writing this chapter, my mind recalled the breathtaking scripture in the book of Psalm 8:3-6. *"What is man that thou art mindful of him?"* What a poignant and thought-provoking question. Of all the living creatures and organisms that the Father created, He created you to have dominion over them all. That alone is a magnanimous thought. Just to know that God had you on His mind during the creation process and chose you to be a part of the segment of His creation that would have dominion and control should open your eyes to the vastness of His love for you. This scripture alone bears witness to the fact that the Father breathed greatness in you from the beginning. However, many have come to the earth forgetting the magnitude of the Father's power that He vested in them. When you truly can grab hold of the greatness of God in you, you will start living and living well.

17

REFRESHING KEY #2
When we live a life of purpose and destiny and we are obedient to the voice of God, it awakens greatness in others.

We have been sent to earth by God to touch and impact lives and to be a catalyst for change, healing and wholeness to manifest in the world. You have been handpicked by God to make a difference in the lives of others. Therefore, it is your God-given responsibility to ask God to show you how to make a difference. You must ask the Father the right questions. When we ask the right questions of the Father and then purpose in our heart to be still and listen, He reveals to us His strategic plan.

How can I touch someone else's life? How can I help my brothers and sisters embrace a greater revelation of God? How can my actions, obedience and results influence others to move in their purpose and fulfill their destiny?

As we live a life of purpose and destiny and we are obedient to the voice of God, it awakens greatness in others. Author Marianne Williamson said, *"As you let your own light shine it motivates others to do the same."* Your obedience will awaken the sleeping giant in someone else and the dreams that were once lying dormant will be resuscitated and revitalized, the gifts and talents that were stagnant will begin to be regenerated and excitement will begin to brew in their lives, all because you chose to do what God has called you to do. You stepped out of your comfort zone and began to live on purpose.

Part of your assignment from the Father is to push someone else to greatness and purpose. While you are on your way to attain why not bring others along with you? Let someone know that they do not have to stay in the negative condition to which they are accustomed. Let them know that there is something better. A better life awaits them. Urge them to reach higher than what their natural eye may see as possible and that there is always something greater for which to reach.

"But whosoever drinketh of the water that I shall give him shall never thirst; but the water that I shall give him shall be in him a well of water springing up into everlasting life." (John 4:14)

Stepping into this awareness and fully embracing that God is in control are times of refreshing from the Father and allows you to sit back and experience the life-giving waters of God. Understanding the nature of God and how He works uniquely in your life will allow you to rid your life of toxic, antiquated thinking, dismiss the negative people around you and empower you to dismantle the thoughts that cause you to feel like you want to quit. There is nothing like drinking the water that will cause you to never thirst again, the water from God Himself.

You Are God's Handiwork

God has chosen each and every one of us for a purpose. He has chosen each and every one of us to fulfill a particular need in the earth. You do not have to duplicate or replicate someone else's anointing. You do not have to run after anyone else's gift. You do not have to walk in the footsteps of anyone else. Your ability to be unique, authentic and true to that which God is asking you to fulfill in the earth will make a vast difference in the world. Your obedience to work your end of the puzzle, your commitment to uphold your end of the bargain, your determination to focus on your corner of the sky will make the difference in this life. As each person is obedient to fulfilling their assignment, the world will be better for all.

The world and the Church are looking for real people - unique but real, different but real, focused on God and giving out only what God says shall be given at the appointed time, not trying to make it greater than what it is or dummy it down. You must be determined to walk in the truth and power of your assignment with boldness and clarity, without hesitation or reservation. Since God created you to be great allow Him to do the rest.

Take a moment to assess all that God has placed inside of you. Take an inventory of the greatness. Assess its worth in your life. Consider its value and ask yourself if 1) you have recognized the hidden treasure that the Father tucked away inside of you; 2) you have begun to bless others with your treasure; and 3) you think it is worth pressing into your purpose so that your hidden treasures can be revealed and others may be empowered, uplifted, inspired and motivated to discover their treasure.

Ask the Creator what it is that He wants you to do with this treasure that He housed on the inside of you so that you don't use it haphazardly, let it lie dormant, let it die, let others discourage you, let anyone douse the fire or let anyone put out your light. All of these things happen in this journey called life. But when we become one with the Father (John 10:30), when we become one with the greatness that God has placed on the inside of us, when we become one with our purpose it is like breathing.

REFRESHING KEY #3
Your commitment to uphold your end of the bargain, your determination to focus on your corner of the sky will make the difference in this life.

I believe that when God breathed the breath of life into Man, into each one of us, it was the same breath but it housed different properties for each individual. Each individual received the greatness that was charged for them. You received the greatness that was charged just for you. The breath that God breathed into you is unique. Therefore, you have to become one with your purpose, your destiny and your assignment. You cannot live by the greatness that was breathed into your mother, your father, your grandparents, siblings, friends or mentors. You have to become one with the Christ that lives in you. You must become true to the existence of the Father in your personal experience.

Greatness is massive when you line it up with who God is. It takes more than just a moment of saying, *"I know what God wants me to do."* It takes more than speaking about your gifts, talents and assignment from God. It takes more than just acknowledging that God has placed greatness in you. It is a process of continually going back to the Creator and asking, *"Father, are you pleased? Do you need me to change the dimensions? Do you need me to change directions? Who do you want me to bless? Am I to go left or right?"*

You must strive for perfection, constantly and consistently trying to perfect your calling to the level of excellence for God. Then and only then will you become one with it and it becomes the thing that you do habitually every day, like eating, sleeping and breathing. You do not have to tell your lungs how to function. Under normal conditions, you do not have to monitor your pancreas on a daily basis to ensure that it is performing. It is just there doing what it was designed to do. Most people do not think about their pancreas unless it fails to function properly and at its optimal level. Likewise, you must become one with your purpose so that you can do the thing that you were created to do. It should not take any prodding, it should not take any extra pushing and no one should have to force you to do it. You just do it because you were born to be great.

Born to be Great

We must tap into the concept that we were born to be great, recognizing that we were put on this earth to do great things. Allow the Spirit of God to take over your body and your mind and begin to push you into greatness. We are living in perilous times, where it is easy to give up. Every day people are being bombarded by one challenge after another. If there were ever a time for excuses to be used to stop us from achieving our greatness, it is now. Interferences, roadblocks, storms, challenges, financial setbacks, foreclosures, unemployment are overtaking the minds of people in this season.

However, when you recognize that you can't breathe without Him, when you recognize that what God has given you in this season of your life is a task for you to complete, then you cannot help but to lay prostrate before Him and say, *"Father, feed me your message. Father, feed me your word. Give me what I need in this hour. Strengthen me."* Petition the Father, as did the man whose son was sick in Mark 9:24, saying, *"Lord, help me with my unbelief."*

REFRESHING KEY #4
Never allow your energy to be depleted for anything other than that which that God created you to do.

If the truth be told, even the strong saints, those who walk around with faith tattooed across their chests and printed on their foreheads can slip into an area of unbelief. The Father knew that the day would come when even you would encounter struggle and doubt and begin to question God. But even in those times you must recognize the vitality of the breath of God, realizing that you cannot breathe without Him and proclaiming, *"Lord, I cannot do anything without you. If it is going to get done, if it is going to happen, it must come through you."*

Faith is the launching pad for our dreams. Constant and consistent faith in the Almighty God is the key to unlock the true essence of God. Faith does not mean that everything will go well every day. But faith says I know God is in everything and whatever is contrary is only temporary. We have to live in that place. It is fruitless to take all the hits that life has to offer and then focus all of your attention, all of your good energy, all of your God-given energy on situations and people that may never ever change. However, the one thing that can change is you.

Work on changing you. Work on being the change that you desire. When you change you, everything else around you changes. When you stop being negative, negative people either change their ways and their conversation or they leave your life. Situations that seem to be pressure cookers for you start to subside, because you no longer focus your attention on them. You no longer give all of your energy to thwarting negativity. Never allow your energy to be depleted for anything other than that which that God created you to do.

It's All About the Kingdom

Jesus says, *"For where two or three are gathered together in my name, there am I in the midst of them."* (Matthew 18:20) It takes strong-minded people who are focused on God to understand the power of this promise. It is not enough to gather together and for everyone to look at each other and say, *"You know the Bible says where two or three gathered together in His name He is in the midst."* It is not a cliché. This promise means something. It signifies power. It signifies strength. Jesus is letting us know that you are a force to be reckoned with.

One reason the world is not changing for the better as quickly as it should and so many people are suffering is that the saints of God have not become one. Denominational differences, belief systems, competition, jealousy, just to name a few, are holding up the blessings for millions of people. There are those who are still holding on to their own personal agendas, trying to figure out how they can achieve success in their own lives before their brother, sister, neighbor, coworker or fellow man.

However, if you should ever drop your guard and allow God to be God in you, you will come to the full revelation that you cannot breathe without Him and we cannot breathe without each other. You cannot manifest greatness on your own. When we come together we are a force to be reckoned with, one force gathered together in His name to manifest greatness and to do great things. If we put our minds together and unite as one and put away our petty differences and personal agendas, together we can move mountains. We will make things happen. We will shake the earth and effectuate change.

We must come together and realize that it is for the good of the Kingdom that we work together and in concert with each other to manifest our individual greatness. It is Kingdom work, Kingdom destiny, Kingdom manifestation. We must fight to be Kingdom-minded and not self-centered. Your focus cannot be on just *your* house, *your* family, *your* business, *your* assignment. Kingdom stretches across your community, your city, your town, your state, your region, across your part of the world. Kingdom is expansive and stretches across the universe. Being Kingdom-minded causes you to realize that you cannot breathe without Him, because the work that the Father has for you to do is massive.

You do not want God to stretch out the blanket of life and discover there is a huge hole, the place that you were assigned to fill, your spot, the thing that you are supposed to do to make this life complete. No one person can do everything. We have to link together and agree to move, and we must acknowledge that each of us individually must motivate, challenge and inspire someone else to do what God has called them to do. Come off of the sidelines. Get off of your bed of affliction. Get your hands dirty. Put your hands to the plow and start doing the thing that God is asking you to do!

However, it takes a different type of mindset than always trying to find excuses for not doing what you were created to do. You can always find excuses for not doing what you have been assigned to do. Yet those excuses, though they may be valid, still do not justify your lack of obedience to God.

REFRESHING KEY #5
Stop waiting and start creating. You will shake the earth and effectuate change.

Earlier you read Susan's story. The key in Susan's story and the key to breakthrough for many is that Susan forgot God created her to be great. Did you forget that God created you to be great? You were born to be great! Do not give up... Press! Be who God created you to be. Many people have forgotten that they were born to be great, countless others have not awakened to the greatness that is living inside of them, and still others have never been told they were great and remain unaware.

We cannot assume that everyone knows and understands the greatness of God within them. Many people are walking around today with undeniable greatness that has been pushed to the background because of the vicissitudes of life. Many young people, middle-aged people, elderly people were never told, *"You were created by God to be great."* Just hearing that truth will turn on the light in someone's spirit.

When you come to the realization that you were born to be great and that greatness lives on the inside of you, then you have the responsibility to share that truth with others. How refreshing it is to see the light bulb illuminate in someone else's life. How refreshing it is to see someone embrace newness in life and begin to live again.

When you are enlightened you must commit to enlighten others. Just the truth that "you were born to be great," can be that defining moment in a person's life that will cause them to take a leap of faith, launch out into the deep and do the thing that God really created them to do. That could be the thing that could cause them to have unspeakable joy. When you embrace your greatness you are being, doing and having everything that God has ordained for you to be, to do and to have in the Earth. We are given an opportunity to constantly remind people that they are great, their destiny is great and their life is great. This act alone should motivate you to continue to forge ahead in power to be all that the Father has created you to be.

God is releasing his Spirit to remind us just how thoughtful He is of us. He gives us the air to breathe. He wakes us up every morning. He protects us. He loves us. Just take time to stop and imagine how powerful God created you to be. Take the time to stop and imagine how great you are. Take the time to stop and breathe and recognize how great and how powerful you are. God is great and the greatness of God is living on the inside of you. Affirm with me, "The greatness of God that is living on the inside of me is going to manifest outside of me, so that everyone around me is affected.

There is absolutely no way you can breathe without Him!

Chapter Two
SOMETIMES YOU HAVE TO STOP
AND EXHALE!

"The spirit of God hath made me, and the breath of the Almighty hath given me life." (Job 33:4)

The Place of Safety

Far too often people allow their day to be dictated by others. Negative words, fear, misunderstandings, worry, sadness and doubt are the culprits to turning a great day (a day that the Lord has made) into a somber, miserable and dreadful day. It is important that you not allow the cares of this world to limit your ability to manifest the greatness that God breathed on the inside of you. You must not allow the pressures of life to hinder your forward movement and stop you from pressing beyond what you see, beyond those things that try to keep you in a limited state. God has birthed greatness on the inside of you. You have to push past the barriers of adversity if you want to break through to the greatness that God has for you.

In this hour, we must hear what God is saying. The world is full of lies and untruths. People have to dig through too much "stuff" just to get to the truth of what God is saying, and by that time they are tired, frustrated and ready to give up. We need to hear truth. We need to speak truth to power so that we can begin to take our rightful place in society.

REFRESHING KEY #6
Every time you exhale you are exhaling greatness into the universe.

Sometimes you have to stop and exhale so that you can understand what God is doing in your life. You have to inhale (take in) what God is saying and exhale (release) the greatness that is on the inside of you out into the earth. You have so much stored up inside of you that sometimes you have to engage in a prophetic act of breathing (inhaling and exhaling into the atmosphere) so that the greatness that God has birthed on the inside of you can live. Remember, "to breathe" means "to be alive; to live." Every time you exhale you are exhaling greatness into the universe.

No matter what challenges you may face you have to exhale and stand on God's promise. You have to be able to stand in the midst of any trial and declare, *"On Christ, the solid rock I stand, all other ground around me is sinking sand."* You can stand on the promises of God. You can rest in the promises of God. There you will find safety. There you can exhale. There you can dream again. There you can live and live well.

The word of God allows you to experience times of refreshing. It builds a fortress. To experience divine protection get inside of the walls of the fortress. It is through prayer, fasting and revelation of the word of God that we start building that fortress. In that fortress God gives divine instruction concerning your purpose and allows you to blow worry to the wind and meditate on His word. It sounds easy, but every day we have to wrestle with the thoughts in our own mind and with the emotions that are in our own heart to keep our eye on what God is saying and His divine plan for our lives.

"For we wrestle not against flesh and blood, but against principalities, against powers, against the rulers of the darkness of this world, against spiritual wickedness in high places."
(Ephesians 6:12)

Worry About No-Thing

"Do not be anxious about anything, but in every situation, by prayer and petition, with thanksgiving, present your requests to God. And the peace of God, which transcends all understanding, will guard your hearts and your minds in Christ Jesus."
(Philippians 4:6-7)

Jesus said in this life we will have trials, we will have struggles, but be of good cheer because He has overcome the world. *"These things I have spoken unto you, that in me ye might have peace. In the world ye shall have tribulation: but be of good cheer; I have overcome the world."* (John 16:33) Worry engulfs us every day. We worry about everything. We worry about our children. We worry about our finances. We worry about our jobs. We worry if we start coughing. We worry if we feel a lump. We worry if we have a sore throat. We worry if someone speaks untruths about us. We worry if we do not have enough money to pay our bills. There are things that cause us to worry day after day after day after day.

Worry is a debilitating emotion. It slowly breaks you down and can incapacitate you. When you first begin to worry you may not feel any effects, but over time worry evolves into depression, sadness, sickness, eating disorders, hair loss, short temperedness, anger and anxiety. It evolves into everything negative. However, you have to work through it because it is a part of the human condition. As soon as an adverse event occurs, worry is often the instantaneous response. It is then that you have to decide whether you are going to gravitate to the side of worry, which is the natural human emotion, or whether you are going to press into Spirit and trust God.

REFRESHING KEY #7
Worry is a debilitating emotion.

There are people who worry for legitimate reasons, and then there are those who worry over that which God has already sent His divine answer. They worry over things for which they have already prayed. Many people also worry about things that God has given to them. They asked God for something, He answered their prayers, but maintaining it is laborious and they are ready to give it back.

In Luke 12:22-26, Jesus commissions us not to worry.

"And he said unto his disciples, 'Therefore I say unto you, Take no thought for your life, what ye shall eat; neither for the body, what ye shall put on. The life is more than meat, and the body is more than raiment. Consider the ravens: for they neither sow nor reap; which neither have storehouse nor barn; and God feedeth them: how much more are ye better than the fowls? And which of you with taking thought can add to his stature one cubit? If ye then be

*not able to do that thing which is least, why take ye thought for the
rest?'"*

There is no need to worry. Bobby McFerrin wrote a song,
Don't Worry, Be Happy. It was a prophetic song that illustrated
what our outlook on life should be. When I thought about the title
I thought about the struggles, the trials and the tribulations that
happen in our lives. If you are not careful they will kill you. You
have to condition yourself to remain in the worry-free zone. You
do not encounter just one struggle, one trial, one situation that
seems to overwhelm you in your lifetime. If that was it, if all you
had to face is one thing and then it happened, you could say, *"at
least I got through that one."* But Jesus said in this life you will
have troubles and trials, situations and struggles. That means that
the whole time that we are here in the earth realm we are going to
have to battle the storms of life, face the tests and overcome
adversity one after the next after the next.

REFRESHING KEY #8
Condition yourself to remain in the worry-free zone.

Those who have never been tested live in a fantasy world.
They live in the illusion that every day is smooth sailing and they
will not encounter opposition. Many Christians believe that just
because they are walking with the Lord they will not face
adversity. They too live in a fantasy world. They look at others
who may be going through a storm and wonder what they have
done wrong in their lives. But keep living. Jesus promised us that
we will have to face some troubles. We cannot choose to believe
some parts of the Bible and ignore other parts. If worry was not a
part of our human nature and was not something that we would

have to contend with every day, then Jesus would not have spoken so much about it in the Scriptures.

When you encounter a storm, often you will hear someone say, *"Don't worry about it, it's going to be okay."* They are just echoing what God already told you. *"If ye then be not able to do that thing which is least, why take ye thought for the rest?"* (Luke 12:26) However, when it looks like calamity is happening all around us, the world is coming to an end, the bottom is falling out of the barrel for some reason it is difficult for many people to comprehend with their human understanding that they do not have to worry. It looks like things are in chaos. They think, *"I have to provide for my family,"* which adds even greater stress.

But Jesus said in Luke 12:29 of the Amplified Bible, *"and do not seek by meditating and reasoning to inquire into..."* Do not ask a lot of questions. Do not try to figure out what is happening. Do not give God a lot of rhetoric in the process. God said, *"Do not seek by meditating and reasoning to inquire into what you are about to eat and what you are going to drink, nor be anxious, troubled, unsettled, excited, worried and in suspense."*

Worry causes anxiety. If you receive a negative report in the mail or an unexpected bill, it can disrupt your whole day and you become anxious and unsettled. You are in suspense because you want to know the outcome, when God said do not worry, you have already won. If we know the end of the story and how it is going to actually play out, when the trial comes we should not be anxious. God does not tell us the details of the process, because He wants us to trust Him. Sometimes He only tells us the beginning and the end of the story. The in between you have to walk by faith. You have to close your eyes and follow Him. It may be a difficult process, but God mandates us not to worry. He has already set it up for you to win.

REFRESHING KEY #9
There are different strategies that God will give us to encounter the process of each storm, but worrying is not one of them.

The trials, storms, tests and challenges are coming, but Jesus already gave us the warning that they will come, therefore, we are able to brace ourselves for the impact. Sometimes when you are driving on the highway you may see orange signs that say, "Bump Ahead." You brace yourself because you know the bumps are coming. You do not continue driving 70 mph. You slow down and prepare for the bumps so that you do not damage your car or cause an accident. During the winter you may see signs that say, "Slippery When Wet." They warn you ahead of time that the road is dangerous so that you can prepare to travel down that road without dying or causing injury to others.

That is what God is saying. *"I'm giving you warning signs. I'm putting orange signs up ahead that there is a bump coming."* When trials come they are like big orange signs warning you to reduce your speed and brace yourself. For each orange sign in the Spirit God has a message for how we are to handle that particular storm, because each storm is different. How are we supposed to handle this particular thing that is coming down the pike? The one thing that we know is that we are not to worry. There are different strategies that God will give us to encounter the process of each storm, but worrying is not one of them.

The Job Effect

In the Bible, Job encountered some storms. He had to work through some challenges. Job was an upright man, but he had to go through some tests. Job was very wealthy and he had a great family, but Job still encountered the storms. It was a custom of his to let his children go out and have fun, and then he sacrificed offerings for them and prayed for them just in case they got off track. But he did not expect to encounter any challenges himself, because he was an upright man and God had given him bountiful blessings. However, in the midst of everything going well, Job encountered the storm and he began to lose everything - his family, his livelihood, his money, everything was taken away.

Have you ever been on the road to "up" and all of a sudden the bottom fell out and you lost everything? You just got out of one financial situation and now you find yourself back in the same place, facing the same problem. Oftentimes, you will try to figure out what went wrong. You may not figure it out. Just know that if you went through it and God delivered you before, He will do it again. Sometimes God will send us through storms just to remind people around us that He is God and that He is the Source. You cannot attribute it to a job. You cannot attribute it to an inheritance. You cannot attribute it to some people who decided they were going to be nice. You must attribute it to the Source.

Sometimes people will try to judge your storm and try to make sense of it. *"How did you get there again? Don't you go to church?"* But when you allow God to work in the midst of your storm he will restore back to you greater than what was taken. Job is a witness. He lost everything, but God gave him double. Job did not lose his trust in God. He went through the human emotion of worry in the process, but he always resorted back to his faith and trust in God. He determined in his heart that he was going to wait for God to change his situation.

"If a man die, shall he live again? all the days of my appointed time will I wait, till my change come." (Job 14:14)

When you allow God to work in the process of your storm, when you go through the trial and endure the test without giving up, God will give you greater and people will know it was God.

REFRESHING KEY #10
Sometimes you have to go up to the next rung of the ladder and have a seat, knowing that God is at work.

You have to fight your flesh. You have to tell your feelings how to feel. In the middle of the test, in the middle of the trial, in the middle of the struggle you have to rest in God. You have to encourage yourself in the storm. You have to refresh yourself in the storm. *"I am not going to worry. I don't have the money for that, but I am not going to panic. I am not going to allow this situation to cause me to become ill."* Sometimes you have to go up to the next rung of the ladder and have a seat, knowing that God is at work.

When you go through the process you can always find something in your life that might be out of order. You can always find something where you think God is not pleased. However, if you know you have been obedient to God, if you know that you have been faithful to God know that God is just showing you another level of His glory.

"Our Father which art in heaven, hallowed be thy name...Give us this day our daily bread." Jesus said when you pray this is how you ought to pray, meaning when you meditate this is what you must say. Do not bring God your bad news. You do not have to tell Him what is happening in your life, because He already knows what you need. He has everything in control. You do not have to give Him a laundry list of your needs. If you tune your ears in to hear Him and not allow stress to clog your life and worry to overwhelm you, then He will send the "raven" to feed you. God sent the raven to feed the prophet Elijah. In 1 Kings 17, God commanded Elijah to go by the brook and God sent a raven there to feed him every day.

"Get thee hence, and turn thee eastward, and hide thyself by the brook Cherith, that is before Jordan. And it shall be, that thou shalt drink of the brook; and I have commanded the ravens to feed thee there."(1 Kings 17:3-4)

God will send you something that you would not expect to feed you. He will send your provision through a vessel that you least expect, and it will appear at your doorstep right at the moment that you need it.

The Final Hour Blessing

You may be going through a storm right now as you are reading this book and it may seem like there is no answer. But at the final hour, God is going to answer your prayer. The final hour can cause you to quit before the blessing makes it to your door. The final hour will cause you to feel like you want to take your last breath because you can no longer take the pressure. The final hour blessing is greater than the pain. However, no matter how many final hour blessings God gives us, we still find ourselves encountering situations and worrying, worrying and wondering, pondering and being in suspense. *"Is the devil attacking my life? Is it God or is it the devil?"* We find ourselves being double-minded, straddling the fence, confused because we face another test, another trial. Nonetheless, if you truly trust God, you will experience the final hour blessing.

Now, those who are not walking upright with God, you need to ask is it God or is it the devil. You need to ask because you are on both sides of the fence. Sometimes it can be the devil wearing you out, sometimes it can be God trying to get your attention. Sometimes it can be the devil saying, *"Aren't we having a great time?"* Sometimes it can be God saying, *"When you have had enough let me know."* But if you are walking upright with God and find yourself facing a storm, know that the final hour blessing is on its way.

REFRESHING KEY #11
If you are going to pray, don't worry.
If you are going to worry, don't pray.

Worry is like a scar on your reactive mind. Worry is a reaction. In order for the scar to be healed you have to be able to pinpoint the object of your reaction. *"Why am I angry? Why am I frustrated?"* The word of God replaces our worry with refreshing thoughts that medicate and heal the scars of the mind. There is a saying, *"If you are going to pray, don't worry. If you are going to worry, don't pray."*

Times of Refreshing

Worry and prayer cannot co-exist. God's word is like medicine. It will heal whatever is ailing you. Accessing God's word is like going into the medicine cabinet and getting what you need for that moment. The word of God medicates the worries and frustrations that we have by reminding us of who we are and what God wants to do in and through our lives. Our minds must be refreshed and renewed. We must get back to the core of what it is that God is doing in our lives.

In God We Trust

"Look at the birds of the air; they do not sow or reap or store away in barns, and yet your heavenly Father feeds them. Are you not much more valuable than they? Can any one of you by worrying add a single hour to your life?" (Matthew 6:25-27)

Trusting God is not a natural human emotion. You have to trust in someone who you cannot see with your natural eye but you know exists and has everything in control. Worry is an instantaneous reaction, unless you train your mind to not worry. The Bible says that we are to be anxious for nothing, but in everything by prayer and supplication make our requests made known. The Bible also says if God can take care of the birds of the air, don't you think he will take care of you, who is greater than the birds. Yet when things begin to happen most people will succumb to that human reaction of worry.

REFRESHING KEY #12
It is when the times appear difficult that your faith is tested.

God is greater than any problem, situation, storm, trial or calamity. You do not have to succumb to the negativity around you. There is always a greater place. You have to condition yourself not to respond to the way your natural man might respond to situations and train yourself to trust God. Retrain your mind to trust God. There are many great spiritual people who say they trust God, but when you dig beneath the layers of their lives you realize they do not really trust God. It is easy to trust God when everything is going well. It is easy to wake up every morning and leap out of the bed when the sun is always shining. However, it is when the times appear difficult that your faith is tested.

God is our Source, and every now and then the Source will remind us that He is the Source. He will allow situations to happen that will cause us to come back to Him (the Source), because He is the way. Anything that gets in between us and Him, He is God enough to remove it. Oftentimes it is difficult to recognize that God is the Source until you lose everything and are forced to live by the Source, the One who you cannot see in the natural, yet He is really making everything happen. God is the Source, but he will always assign a person to release your provision. God uses people to release His blessings to His children. When God wants to test your faith He will remove the faces of people and force you to trust Him, whom you cannot see with your natural eye.

It is a fight to trust God. You can preach it, proclaim it, prophesy it and declare it, but God will always put you to the test in front of a people who will say, *"I thought you said that God was*

41

your source?" If you proclaim how great God is and you encourage other people to trust God even in the difficult times, God will put you to the test. He will call you to the carpet. He will test your faith and your willingness to live by His word. Your trust is put to the test when you look at people whose lives are out of order and they appear to have no worries, yet you are doing everything that God asked you to do and it seems like your life is topsy-turvy. It is in those moments that that you have to demonstrate that you truly trust God.

Not With Human Hands

"God that made the world and all things therein, seeing that he is Lord of heaven and earth, dwelleth not in temples made with hands; Neither is worshipped with men's hands, as though he needed any thing, seeing he giveth to all life, and breath, and all things; And hath made of one blood all nations of men for to dwell on all the face of the earth, and hath determined the times before appointed, and the bounds of their habitation; That they should seek the Lord, if haply they might feel after him, and find him, though he be not far from every one of us:"
(Acts 17:24-27)

Are you feeling refreshed? Are you feeling encouraged? Our ability to trust God through the process of life gives us the ability to breathe, to inhale His goodness and to exhale His greatness, knowing that the Father has everything in control. It is in that moment that you can hear the still, small voice of God. You can hear His small voice even in the midst of the noise that is blaring in your life.

When you focus on the breath, the noise around you is silenced and you can hear God speaking in the midst of the storm saying, *"Don't worry, I have it all under control. I know you want to panic, but I am working it out. I know that you want human intervention here so that things can work out, but I want to do the supernatural. If you trust me, I will do greater than any man could do with human hands."*

When supernatural comes, let supernatural work, because it will work so much better than natural. Natural may soothe you for a moment, but if you need a supernatural response to a natural occurrence, let God do it. The key is to allow God to put you in the proper place and space that only He ordains. When you are in in the midst of the storm and in need of God's divine intervention, God will use you to help someone through their storm. He will challenge you to take your eyes off of your situation and place your attention on someone else, knowing that He is working on your situation.

That is true faith, putting your cares on the back burner and giving your attention to someone else. When you are going through a trial do not sit and waddle in your own challenge, but step out, trust God and help someone else. God will supernaturally intervene in your life and provide your every need.

REFRESHING KEY #13
When you focus on the breath, the noise around you is silenced and you can hear God speaking in the midst of the storm.

"Therefore I say unto you, Take no thought for your life, what ye shall eat, or what ye shall drink; nor yet for your body, what ye

shall put on. Wherefore, if God so clothe the grass of the field, which to day is, and to morrow is cast into the oven, shall he not much more clothe you, O ye of little faith?" (Matthew 6:25 and 30)

Never waver in your trust in God, for a double-minded man is unstable in everything that he does. (James 1:8) In the midst of your tests and storms and trials you must muster the ability to leap every hurdle. It is a true reflection that when God promises you something you can stand on His promise. Human hands can never manifest what God's supernatural power can manifest in your life. God's hand is powerful. If God said it, believe it. When you stand on His promises, do not move to the left or to the right, do not look for other options, do not conjure up a Plan B, just stand. Do not pick up the rock and move it to another place and stand on it. Stand right where He said.

"Therefore whosoever heareth these sayings of mine, and doeth them, I will liken him unto a wise man, which built his house upon a rock: And the rain descended, and the floods came, and the winds blew, and beat upon that house; and it fell not: for it was founded upon a rock." (Matthew 7:24-25)

The songwriter, Edward Mote wrote...

My hope is built on nothing less
Than Jesus' blood and righteousness;
I dare not trust the sweetest frame,
But wholly lean on Jesus' name.

On Christ, the solid Rock, I stand;
All other ground is sinking sand,

What looks like a dirty piece of coal one moment becomes a shiny diamond the next moment, if you can trust God and wait on Him. It may not look that way. Your hands may get dirty, your knees may get dirty, your face may get dirty, but underneath, when you dig deep enough there is greatness. In order for us to win in this game called life, we must be able to withstand any test, endure any trial, weather any storm and stand in the midst of the rain. When you are able to stand and not give up, when you are able to persevere in the face of adversity, when you are able to hold your head up high even in the face of embarrassing moments you increase your strength and fortitude to win and God gets the glory.

Isn't your God greater than any devil or any enemy or any bad report? My answer is yes! What is your answer? Our God is so much greater. It docs get better. If you can exhale into the greater, greater will manifest and you will experience greater in your natural experience.

Chapter Three
WHO ARE YOU?

"The Lord will make you the head, not the tail. If you pay attention to the commands of the Lord your God that I give you this day and carefully follow them, you will always be at the top, never at the bottom." (Deuteronomy 28:13)

*L*isa was a secretary of a major computer programming firm, yet she herself was a computer programmer at heart. She had a passion for her work and put her heart into every project that she was given. However, Lisa was always passed by when higher level positions became available at her company. She was never the one picked for the promotion. Although she knew how to do the high level programming, she was never chosen to advance beyond her administrative position. She was always overlooked. Every day after work, Lisa would study the various projects that her boss and the other programmers were working on and would dream and strategize about the way she would complete the projects.

Lisa was considered a genius by many. In school she excelled. She was always at the top of her class. However, Lisa ran into some pitfalls in life. She always found herself in the company of those who downplayed her skill level. Even in her position as secretary, the staff treated her as if she did not understand the higher level information. Lisa was quiet by nature, and as a result, she frequently found herself in the company of people who made her feel like she was "less than."

As Lisa matured in life she began to believe the lies that people told her. She never pursued higher education or higher level positions. She <u>settled</u> for the administrative positions. She often found herself shrinking in the presence of others and retreating to the background. Yet Lisa was always studying in secret, creating and designing new, innovative programs.

One day, Lisa was speaking to a friend who told her that she needed to be introduced to the "real Lisa." She was told that greatness was inside of her, that she needed to tap into who God created her to be and begin to walk in her true identity. Lisa needed to take a moment and introduce herself to the real Lisa!

I have a question for YOU... Are you living according to the label that man has placed on you, or are you living according to who God created you to be?

The issues that Lisa faced could be resolved if she was able to think differently, get rid of the fear, let go of the heavy baggage of negativity and stop allowing people to define her. Can you relate to Lisa's story? Are you holding on to some baggage that you have refused to let go over the years? Are you constantly trying to please others? Have you settled for less than the best that God has for you?

The negative words of others can build a fortress of doubt, fear, depression and sadness, trapping you in the "land of limitation." Never allow people to speak contrary to the greatness that God so carefully crafted within you... Remember, you are the Father's masterpiece!

"For we are God's handiwork, created in Christ Jesus to do good works, which God prepared in advance for us to do."
(Ephesians 2:10)

God has a tremendous plan for your life. He has given you dominion over the earth from the foundation of the world. The same God that created the universe placed His Spirit within you. As a result, you have the same creative abilities and characteristics as the Father. How awesome is that? What an amazing God! You have an obligation to your Heavenly Father to represent Him well!

REFRESHING KEY #14
Don't pick up the rock and move it to another place and stand on it. Stand right where He said!

Why Am I Here?

Many Christians ask the popular questions, *why am I here? What is my purpose? What is my assignment from the Father?* As you stop taking life for granted and acknowledge what God is doing in your life, you will realize that your life does have meaning and purpose. It is very sad when the members of the body of Christ do not fully express themselves in the earth the way that God ordained. They allow the cares of this world to set them back, to erect barriers of limitation and to cause depression and defeat just because their day did not go as planned or someone cut them off on the highway or someone got in line ahead of them. However, until you get a full understanding of why you are here and your purpose in this life, you will live a very frustrated life.

"I will praise thee; for I am fearfully and wonderfully made: marvellous are thy works; and that my soul knoweth right well."
(Psalm 139:14)

God created each of us to be unique in our own special way. God created us to be different. It is very dangerous to model your life after someone else if you are not secure in who you are, and if you do not know your individual assignment from the Father, because if someone disappoints you it can disrupt your world.

REFRESHING KEY #15
Tap in! Really tap in and zero in on your purpose.

It is like the athlete. Everyone loves the talented athlete whose life appears to be perfect. But as soon as he or she does something that is out of their character people become disappointed. They put too much stock in his/her life and not enough stock in their own lives. If you are not aware of who you are and cognizant of the person God created you to be and the divine assignment the Father gave to you, frailties, weaknesses, deficiencies and lack of wisdom will cause you to be in search of a "hero" to rescue you from your present state. You will search for that "perfect person" who looks like they have their life in order and everything is going well and you will strive to be like them. You will emulate their walk, you will emulate their talk, you will emulate their dress until you no longer know who you are and you become the imposter.

If you fail to recognize who you really are, you will always fall short of who God created you to be. It is when we begin to understand who we are in Him that we become empowered to manifest our purpose. We were created to worship Him. We were created to reflect the glory of God through the good times and through the challenging times.

You must tap into the reason why the Father sent you to the earth realm; if not you, will live your life in a state of discontentment. You will never feel satisfied. You will never feel refreshed. You have to seek God diligently concerning your life. *"Father, tell me why you created me. Allow me to zero in on my purpose."* You have to have tunnel vision for a season to get an understanding of your purpose, your assignment and your destiny. Although everything that the Father reveals to you may not seem to come together in your natural experience at one time, you will be able to recognize pieces of the puzzle as God brings them to you and you will better understand the different seasons in your life. You will not faint and become weary. You will not become discouraged when the storms of life rage. You will not give up at the first sign of trouble. *"And let us not be weary in well doing: for in due season we shall reap, if we faint not."* (Galatians 6:9)

David said, *"I had fainted, unless I had believed to see the goodness of the LORD in the land of the living."* (Psalm 27:13) Understanding your purpose and who God created you to be allows you to encounter the storms, but not panic, faint, worry or fear, knowing that you will see the goodness of the Lord and that everything is working together for your good.

Let It Shine

"Let your light so shine before men, that they may see your good works, and glorify your Father which is in heaven."
(Matthew 5:16)

51

We were created to worship the Father. Therefore, we have to make available in our hearts the space to be able to worship Him constantly and consistently. Our lives should honor the Father for creating us with purpose. We have to channel our emotions in the right direction so that we can magnify Him even in the midst of what looks like calamity. You were created to worship, to magnify, to bring glory to your Heavenly Father in the good times (when it is evident that God is moving in your life) and in the difficult times. Your mind, your heart and your emotions must be set on worshipping the Father, because only you know God's purpose for sending you to the Earth.

REFRESHING KEY #16
Channel your emotions in the right direction - towards the Father not the problem.

Many people are letting their light shine, but their good works are not seen. Many people are hurting in this hour, even those in the body of Christ. Many are experiencing devastation and calamity in their lives and are succumbing to the pressures of life because their eyes are not fixed on the right solution (Jesus Christ). They are focused on the problem. They are focused on their condition. They are more focused on the pain than the promise. They emit energy of defeat, which causes others to feel uncomfortable in their presence. Their light is not reflecting their good works. Their light is not shining so that their Father is glorified. Regardless of what you may encounter from moment to moment, from day to day, whether good, bad or indifferent, your life must still reflect the glory of God.

Even in the midst of your storm you must let your light shine, because it is a testament that you trust God. It is a testament that your God is greater than any storm. If you can trust God in the midst of the storm, you have tapped into the kingdom and you are committed to handling the Father's business. The issues of the world should not break your focus. They should not sideline you. God will not sit you on the bench. He will not put you out of the game. The Father encourages us to press toward the mark even amidst the most adverse conditions.

The Apostle Paul said, *"Brethren, I count not myself to have apprehended: but this one thing I do, forgetting those things which are behind, and reaching forth unto those things which are before, I press toward the mark for the prize of the high calling of God in Christ Jesus."* (Philippians 3:13-14)

Although God will never put you out of the game, if you are not focused on the reason God created you and if you do not know who you are, the situations of life can become so overwhelming that you sideline yourself. You will find every reason to quit because everything is not lining up according to the perfect world that the Father showed you.

However, when you live in God's world, His world is perfect. Perfection in the eyes of God may not be as you perceive. It may not be Webster's definition of perfection. On the other hand, you may be misinterpreting the definition. God's world is the epitome of perfection. *"And the light shineth in darkness; and the darkness comprehended it not."* (John 1:5)

REFRESHING KEY #17
When you live in God's world His world is perfect.

You may imagine the perfect world or what you perceive the perfect world to be, but God will use everything that you go through in life to reflect His glory. He will let your light shine in the midst of darkness. He will call forth light out of your dark places. Some experiences you encounter may look like the hand of the devil, but God will use that experience to reveal His glory through you.

Have you had a very troubled past? Have you battled with bad habits and limiting beliefs that have caused you to be confused about your purpose? It is time to be introduced to the real you. It is time to be introduced to the One who created you. It is time for your light to shine so that people may see your good works.

If you purchase a BMW automobile and it begins to malfunction, the best person to repair the car is the manufacturer. The manufacturer knows how the car was made. The manufacturer knows every intricate detail of the car. The same is true for your Heavenly Father who created you. If you are unsure of who you are and your purpose, you must go back to the Creator so that He can reveal to you the intricate details of His creation. Your whole life will change. That which you did in the past you will no longer do, because you know the intricate details of your life as revealed by the Creator. Instead, you will use your trials as fuel to move forward. In the midst of your storm, God is still creating. In the midst of your trial, God is still perfecting you.

Are You Available?

"Set your affection on things above, not on things on the earth." (Colossians 3:2)

You have to make space in your mind and in your heart for that which God wants to do in you. You have to give the Holy Spirit the available space that is necessary to dwell within you and exercise His power in and through you. Give yourself permission to do exactly what God has destined you to do. Many people give themselves permission in this life, but unfortunately, they give themselves permission to accept the wrong things. They give themselves permission to be depressed, unhappy, frustrated, angry, disappointed, fearful and anxious, all of which take up the available "God space" and they engage in the acts, efforts and activities that do not attribute to the greatness and power of God in their lives.

Make room for God and give Him the available space necessary in your life so that Matthew 5:16 can become real in your life. When your light shines before men it reaches places before you get there and people can see it from afar. The songwriter wrote, *"Lord I am available to you."* When you are in the midst of a storm you have to declare, Lord, I am available to you. You have to speak the right language to the storm. You have to speak a language that affirms God is in control. Do not allow the storm to overwhelm you. Develop your vocabulary to speak to the storm and cause the storm to cease in your life.

"For verily I say unto you, That whosoever shall say unto this mountain, Be thou removed, and be thou cast into the sea; and

shall not doubt in his heart, but shall believe that those things which he saith shall come to pass; he shall have whatsoever he saith. " (Mark 11:23)

REFRESHING KEY #18
Develop your vocabulary to speak to the storm and cause the storm to cease in your life.

Speak to your storm - *"Lord, I am available."* Speak to your storm - *"Be thou removed and cast into the sea!"* Speak to your storm - *"Storm cease!"* Tell the storm that you are available to God and God alone, not to trouble, heartache or devastation. When you declare that you are available to God, fear, worry and anxiety leave you, creating that available space in your heart and mind. Rid yourself of the detractors of your spirit - depression, frustration sadness, anxiety and disappointment.

Disappointment disrupts your life and causes you not to focus on the important things in life, those things that will allow you to express the true nature of who you are. Disappointment has sidelined many people. Disappointment causes you to feel like you have missed an appointment. But can you really miss God's appointment?

Disappointment occupies a vast space in your heart and mind, if you allow it - disappointment in people, disappointment in areas of your life that you have not yet succeeded in, setting expectations for something to happen that do not manifest the way you imagined. However, we should only put our complete trust in

God. Only God is the same yesterday, today and forever. (Hebrews 13:8) Man's actions are subject to change.

If God makes you a promise, you can live in great expectation for God to do exactly what He promised. *"For all the promises of God in him are yea, and in him Amen, unto the glory of God by us."(*2 Corinthians 1:20) God always keeps His promise. If He made you a promise, then you can live in expectation until you see the manifestation thereof. If you stay focused, if you say, *"Lord, I'm available,"* if you learn to speak to your storm, then you will not allow man to disappointment you.

The reason why many people are confused about their true identity and their purpose in life is that they are unfulfilled. They have allowed themselves to be disappointed. They have not made the available space for God. They have not relinquished their lives to Him. Many people prefer to hold on to negative people, negative ideologies, negative thoughts and negative belief systems, the very things that are not expressing the true God that is living on the inside of them, and as a result they express everything that is not of God. They focus their attention on the things that will cause them not to succeed in life.

REFRESHING KEY #19
Proclaim today, "Lord, I am available for your service."

As you agree with God and affirm who you are, the person God created you to be, your mind changes. It only takes one word to change you and put you on track and in tune with what God has for you. As you affirm, *"Lord, I'm available"* you give yourself power and permission to become great. You give yourself power to declare that everything around you that is outside of the Father's will and plan for your life does not belong there, because you are available to God and God alone. Tap yourself and say with me, *"This space is for God. My life is for God."*

This mindset will shift you to a new level in God. It will cause you to not miss the mark. As you continue to affirm your availability to God, suddenly you will find that it is greater than the disappointment. Your availability to God is greater than the depression. Your availability to God is greater than the sickness. For the next 30 days, wake up each day affirming, *"Lord, I'm available to you."* Continually speak these words until they become your reality and those very words will become the light that shines before men.

It's Impossible to Lose

"The steps of a good man are ordered by the LORD: and he delighteth in his way. Though he fall, he shall not be utterly cast down: for the LORD upholdeth him with his hand."
(Psalm 37:24-25)

If you really want to tap into your God-purpose and fulfill your God-ordained destiny, you must focus on winning. Whatever causes you to lose must be cast aside. Let every situation that you encounter, whether good, bad or indifferent, cause you to become better and better, not bitter and bitter. If you continue to strive for what God has for you, you will thrive. You will succeed. You will be on top. You will win. Never allow the storms of life to continually sideline you and thrust you back to point A. You have to allow your storm to catapult you to a greater level. Do not wait until the storm is over to try to recover.

Allow the storm to catapult you to your next level and into your next season, because that is what the storm was designed to do. There is always calm after a storm. Therefore, do not anticipate catastrophe after the storm. Anticipate the calm and shift yourself there even in the midst of the storm. You must be proactive in your recovery. Seek the face of God in the midst of the storm, affirm your true identity, cast down every negative imagination that does not align with your God-nature and trust that you are safe in the arms of the Father.

REFRESHING KEY #20
Don't just sit there and take a hit. Be proactive in your recovery.

Some people may say it does not take all of that. But when you are fighting to manifest purpose and destiny in your life it takes all of that and then some. Those who say it does not take all of that have not gone beyond their own limitations. They have not allowed God to stretch them during their trials. They have not really worked their faith. Instead of fighting, they give in to adversity and settle for less than what God has for them. Once you stop seeing yourself as small you will realize that there is nothing that you cannot accomplish.

"And the LORD shall make thee the head, and not the tail; and thou shalt be above only, and thou shalt not be beneath; if that thou hearken unto the commandments of the LORD thy God, which

I command thee this day, to observe and to do them:"
(Deuteronomy 28:13)

Become one with the words in Deuteronomy 28:13, as this scripture defines who you really are. You cannot proclaim that God created you to be the head and not the tail, if you do not fully understand what the scripture means or if you really do not believe it. Many people affirm, *"I am the head and not the tail; I am above and not beneath,"* but they do not tap into the power of the meaning.

What is God saying to us? God said we are the head. We are first. We are on top. We have dominion. Then why do so many people fight to be the tail? There are those who unconsciously fight to be the tail every day. You have to be consciously aware that you are fighting the right fight. 1 Timothy 6:12 says we must *"fight the good fight of faith."* When you succumb to depression and disappointment, sadness, fear, lack, poverty, low self-esteem, you are fighting to be the tail. Sometimes people unconsciously fight to be the tail, unconsciously fight be inferior, unconsciously fight to be in poverty.

When you realize just how great you are and value the breath that the Father breathed into you, you will take your rightful position in the earth. You will no longer accept the "beneath" position. You will come from the back of the line. God gave us dominion over everything. We just have to learn how to till the ground that he has given to us. I realize that it takes a lot of effort. You cannot till the ground today and sit down tomorrow. You cannot till the ground this year and next year decide to quit because of confusion and disappointment. You have to allow yourself to go from level to level, from faith to faith, from glory to glory in God. How? By putting your focus and your mental energy on the Father, recognizing who He says that you are and recognizing who He is in your life.

As you let your light shine before men it is another way of saying that you are producing something. It is another way of saying that you have fruit on your tree. It gives you the confidence and the boldness to be able to testify to the tremendous things that God is doing in your life. It is your opportunity to share the goodness and the mercy that God has granted to you with others who may be struggling. If God put you in the garden and commanded you to till the ground and care for it, then it is obvious that he does not see you as the tail. He does not see you as beneath. He does not see you as small. The Father sees your greatness.

REFRESHING KEY #21
Come from the back of the line and take your rightful position in God.

You have to make sure you are in the right line. Many people stand in the wrong line and do not realize it until they have stood there for an exorbitant amount of time. The line is long so they assume it is the right line. They are unaware that two aisles over someone is waving their hands saying, *"I'm open."* They are practically jumping up and down for you to see their line is empty. Sometimes you have to come out of the wrong line and get in the right line.

I have listened to young people in their early 20's, whose lives have barely started, who have already given up on life. They refuse to go to school. They refuse to strive for a better life. I always ask the question, *"Who taught you to fight to be the tail?"* God created them to have dominion, yet they fight for the scraps, they fight for the leftovers, they fight for what is not important. If your circumstances and surroundings dictate that you are last and that you are the tail, if you are not aware, you will unconsciously fall into that mode. You must awaken from your slumber. Do you realize that you are fighting to be behind? God never created you to live beneath or behind. God said the first shall be last and the last shall be first. (Matthew 20:16)

SPEAK LIFE!

Tap into your God-power and begin to shift yourself into a new position in life. Only you have the power to do that. You have to make up in your mind that you are God's child, an heir of His promises! When you tap into the real you and begin to operate at your highest potential you will feel stronger, powerful, motivated, encouraged and excited about life. Not only that, you will raise the bar in how people view you and people will begin to treat you like you should be treated. Why? Because you decided to let go of the baggage of negativity, take your rightful position in life and proclaim that you will no longer take the back seat to anyone ever again!

WELCOME TO THE NEW YOU!

Chapter Four
YOU GOT TO FIGHT TO WIN!

"Fight the good fight of faith, lay hold on eternal life, to which you were also called and have confessed the good confession in the presence of many witnesses." (1Timothy 6:12)

Did you know that God has already equipped you with every good thing that you need to win in this life? Did you know that everything that you need to manifest the purpose and plan of God in your life has already been placed within you and it has been there since the beginning of time? The Father has already equipped you with everything that you need to be victorious in this lifetime. It is the Father's good pleasure to give you the kingdom! (Luke 12:32)

In this day and age you have to fight to win!

You may be facing a dilemma right now. The enemy may be trying his best to get you to bow down to the contrary conditions that are facing you. Many obstacles and trap doors may have even been erected in your path. The enemy of your soul would love to see you curse God and die, because the enemy knows that if he can cause you to doubt for one moment, your faith will fail.

Oftentimes, the cares and stresses of life will have us think that contrary conditions are not working out in our favor. You may feel that you do not have enough money, enough resources, enough support or even enough people agreeing with you to manifest the promises of God in your life. But the devil is a liar! All things are working together for your good, even right now! Whatever trials you are facing, whatever storms you are walking through, whatever tests are ahead of you know that God is working in and through each and every one of them to bring you to His expected end. (Jeremiah 29:11) Count it all joy!

"My brethren, count it all joy when ye fall into divers temptations; Knowing this, that the trying of your faith worketh patience. But let patience have her perfect work, that ye may be perfect and entire, wanting nothing." (James 1:2-4)

The enemy may be trying to pull everything from his arsenal against you because he is convinced that you are defeated and just about ready to throw in the towel. But I have some good news! God said, do not give up! Just as God delivered the children of Israel out of Egypt, He will deliver you out of your situation. And guess what? It is not going to take 40 years to get the job done. God said, "Tell my people they have to fight to win!" God wants you to know that you are a winner! The victory is already yours! Success is already yours! Manifestation is already yours! However, you just have to trust God and walk out the process.

REFRESHING KEY #22
The Father has already equipped you with everything that you need to be victorious in this lifetime!

You cannot give up. You cannot throw in the towel. You cannot allow the pressures of life to overwhelm you. If you are able to stand in the midst of whatever is happening in your life right now, knowing that God has already told you that **YOU WIN**, then you will experience the hand of God moving in your life like never before, and yes, peace will be your portion. The question is do you believe it?

What Are You Fighting?

Many people fight in life and have no clue why they are fighting. They fight their families, their bosses, their friends, their enemies. Sometimes they fight because everyone else is fighting, yet they themselves gain nothing as a result. They go with the flow of the crowd without understanding the issues within the crowd. This behavior is very similar to the "mob psychology." The mob psychology is the idea that people desire oneness within a group, and as a result they lose their individual identity and go along with the flow of the crowed. For example, a fight can ensue in a crowd and people will engage in the fight before they know the cause for which they are fighting. Their need to be a part of a group may overshadow their individual beliefs, morals, principles and even God's plan for their lives. Oftentimes, they fail to understand who God created them to be.

When you are aware of who God is in you, you will fight against anything that tries to occupy the available space that is designated for God. The Bible says that we should fight the "good fight of faith." As we discussed in the previous chapter, many people go from relationship to relationship, person to person constantly fighting the spirit of disappointment. I have witnessed many people break very good relationships because they were disappointed. They expected something that they did not receive. However, you cannot put the expectations of God on man, because man is not God. Man is subject to change. If you set expectations for man and govern your life according to those expectations, you run the risk of being disappointed every day.

Have you put your dreams on the shelf? Have you suppressed your fervor for God? Have you chosen to not do what God is asking you to do because someone disappointed you? Do not allow man to cause you to miss your appointment with God. If you were in a relationship that ended abruptly, that does not mean that your appointment with God has ended. It means that you have to open your eyes and see what God is doing in your life. Disappointment, if not resolved, will breed discontentment, which will result in frustration, sickness and anger. You can wake up in a good mood, everything in the day could be going well, step into an environment that is full of frustration and anger and suddenly your mood changes. Why? You have given your available space over to the wrong spirit.

REFRESHING KEY #23
God works everything together for your good!

You must eradicate the spirit of disappointment. Disappointment blocks you from manifesting the greatness that God has placed in you and instead you will manifest unforgiveness and lack. You will find yourself spiraling downward and eventually falling into a state of depression. You may have encountered some devastating situations in your childhood and the memories are still painful even as an adult. God works everything together for your good.

What you had to endure may not have been good, but thank God for grace. Thank God for who you are today. Thank God for allowing you to understand that your available space belongs to Him. Thank God for giving you the understanding that your light should shine before men so that he can be glorified. Give God glory and thanks that you did not allow it to stop you from achieving your greatness.

Everyone has a story. Everyone has an excuse to give up. One person's story may sound worse than someone else's story, but the end result is the same - negativity. The question is why are you giving your available space to negativity? Let's turn it around. Those who are moving and striving for greater in this life, all they did was turn it around. You can turn it around. One way to turn it around is to monitor your mental and emotional temperature throughout the day. Regulate your thought process throughout the day. Failure to regulate your thought process can result in disappointment and depression. It will cause you to think about a situation that happened 10 years ago and be disappointed all over again as if it just happened.

Don't allow disappointment to grab you by the ankles and stop you from moving. Don't allow depression to put a chokehold around your neck and cause you to stop breathing, moving and doing what God has created you to do. Don't allow anything to cause you to relinquish that available space for God. Don't allow anything to thwart the plan of God for your life and cause you say, *"Depression, you can live here; sadness, you can live here; sickness, go ahead and reside here. This space was available for God, but I am going to allow you to take that space."*

REFRESHING KEY #24
Don't allow anything to thwart the plan of God for your life!

It is high time you realize just how great God is. Evict the "tenants" that are taking up God's space within you, those tenants who are living within you rent free. They are occupying your space, but they did not pay to get there. Jesus paid it all. Therefore, all of the space belongs to God. He should be able to have all of you. Get rid of the squatters - depression, sadness, disappointment, sickness and anything that can cause you to justify not doing what God has called you to do.

Cast it Down!

"(For the weapons of our warfare are not carnal, but mighty through God to the pulling down of strong holds;) Casting down imaginations, and every high thing that exalteth itself against the knowledge of God, and bringing into captivity every thought to the obedience of Christ." (2 Corinthians 10:4-5)

The Bible says we are to hold our thoughts captive. There are a lot of negative thoughts that we allow to run free in our lives. We must begin to grab those thoughts that try to rob us of a good day. You can be having a great day, and all it takes is that one moment, that one situation to cause you to think that out of the 24 hours in a day, what happened in 10 minutes just ruined the entire 24 hour period. I refuse to give 10 minutes of a day more power than the other 23 hours and 50 minutes that God has given me. Do not allow 10 minutes to distract you from what God wants to do in your life. If negative things are overtaking you, cast them down!

If you allow junk to reside in you, there will be no room to do what God is asking you to do. You do not want to be at a place where you have no room for God. The songwriter wrote, *"My storage is empty and I am available."* What are you storing within you? Some people have such horrible memories in their storage that they are unable to be available for God. If you love God, what are you doing for Him? Are you doing what He asked you to do? Are you doing what He created you to do?

You may have a small closet in your kitchen that you use for storing your canned goods. Whenever you want a vegetable, you go to the storage and pull it out. If you are storing negativity in your storage, all you can draw is negativity. If you want anger, then you go to the storage room and pull out the anger. If you want to be frustrated, go there and pull out the frustration. However, when you open that cupboard and you find that there is no disappointment in there, there is no lack in there, there is no depression in there, there is no sickness in there, but all you find is the mind of God, the peace of God, the power of God, the joy of the Lord, then you know that you have overcome.

REFRESHING KEY #25
You have a right to refuse anything negative that comes your way!

Many people find it difficult to get in the presence of God, but they gravitate to negativity very quickly - anger, disappointment, fear. It's almost a natural response. *"Are we fighting? Where is the fight? I am ready to go."* They are so quick to engage in the negative that they do not realize that their storage is empty of God's presence and full of the enemy's schemes, plans and devices - everything that causes you to lose in life. This is the result of not understanding the purpose for which God has placed you in the earth.

You may not fully understand why you are here, but one thing is for certain, you are not here to manifest negativity, hatred, disappointment, lack, fear, sadness or depression. You are not here to create havoc, discontentment and confusion. You are not here to help destroy the lives of others. What is your purpose? What is your light that God wants to shine before men? Everyone's light is different. By divine law you have a right to refuse anything negative that comes your way. You do not have to accept it, not one day, not one hour, not one second. Cast it out!

If you know you are carrying squatters on board in your storage and you are not allowing yourself to be fully available so that you can manifest everything that God has placed in you, get rid of them. Get rid of the junk in your storage. Strive toward the perfection of God.

"But we have this treasure in earthen vessels, that the excellency of the power may be of God, and not of us."
(2 Corinthians 4:7)

The definition of perfection is, *"the state of being free; as free as possible from all flaws and defects."* In God everything is perfect. You cannot, with your natural eye, try to evaluate perfection. God has given us everything that we need to manifest, everything that we need to have unspeakable joy, everything that we need for divine health, everything that we need to be in order with God. We just have to dig for the treasure.

We have this treasure in earthen vessels, within us, but we have to dig to discover it. No matter what it looks like in your natural, you must keep digging and digging and digging. You have to dig through the hurt, dig through the pain, dig through the disappointment. You will have to dig through adversity, challenges and negative people. Nevertheless, the more you dig the more you will see the perfection of God. Then you will know that you are free.

The perfection of God represents the Spirit of God. *"Now the Lord is that Spirit: and where the Spirit of the Lord is, there is liberty."* (2 Corinthians 3:17) Where there is liberty there is freedom. Whom the son has set free is free indeed. You know you are moving in perfection when you are moving and walking by the Spirit of God, totally and completely free. You know that you are free when in the midst of a storm you can still declare, Lord, I'm available. You know that you are free when you encounter the most negative situations and you do not allow your mind to dwell there. When you are faced with tragedy dig for the treasure within and stay focused there. If God delivered you once, he will surely do it again. You just have to change your perspective.

Don't Wait Another Second!

"The soul of the sluggard desireth, and hath nothing: but the soul of the diligent shall be made fat." (Proverbs 13:4)

Could it be that the reason we do not have all that God has promised is that another squatter is on board? Procrastination causes us to say, "I will do it tomorrow." Procrastination haunts people every day at different levels. You can find many different

71

reasons for not doing what God has created you to do. You can find a plethora of reasons for not working on your purpose. However, the main reason goes back to what we were just discussing - disappointment: disappointment that you tried it before and it didn't work; disappointment that you didn't get the money when you thought you were supposed to get it; disappointment that you didn't get the promotion; disappointment that someone went ahead of you and it was not fair. We have so many excuses to justify our inability and unwillingness to tap into the greatness that God has for us.

REFRESHING KEY #26
Procrastination robs you of who you are in God!

Procrastination stops you from doing. It can be a major stronghold in your life. It is the enemy trying to stop you, causing you to put off into the future something that you can do in the present. The way to combat procrastination is to take action now. As you feel that sense of, *"I'll do it tomorrow, in an hour, later,"* carry out the task right away. You will find that it takes less time to do the task than it does to keep putting it off.

How many people said I am going to get my degree next year and seven years later they could have had two degrees, yet they are still saying I am going to get my degree? Procrastination! It robs you of your future! We have to fight to break free from it. If it were easy to do what God called us to do, everyone would be doing it. You have to break free. Procrastination comes like a thief in the night. It doesn't knock. It will subtly come in and take residence within you and you may never realize that it is there.

You have to force yourself to make strides toward your destiny. You have to force yourself to leap the hurdles. You have to force yourself to stay in the race! If you don't do it, it will not get done, and before you know it you will talk yourself out of the promise and right out of the will of God for your life. If you want to be a high achiever, you must fight through procrastination. You have to step up to the next level. Otherwise, procrastination will remain in your storage and will give way 10 years later to disappointment. You have to fight for greatness.

Let your prayer be, *"Lord, kick out the squatters. Kick them out so that my storage can be empty and I can be available to do everything that you have called me to do."* You are able to kick out the squatters whenever you are ready for them to leave. You have the power!

Do you believe you are a winner?

Do you believe you already have the victory?

Do you believe that which God has already promised you will manifest?

You are already a winner, but you have to fight to win! You have to fight negativity. You have to fight your own contrary thoughts. You have to fight the disheartening unbelief of others. Stand in front of a mirror and say, "I AM A WINNER!" Victory is in your mouth. You just have to have the boldness and the courage to speak victory in the face of adversity. You have to look those negative, contrary, but oh, so temporary situations in the face and declare… **I WIN!**

REFRESHING AFFIRMATION:

Lord, let me live in you and you live in me. Allow me to cast my cares upon you, for I know that you care for me. I know that you are with me. Thank you Father, for doing it again in my life!

Chapter Five
VICTORY OVER TEMPTATION

"Blessed (happy, to be envied) is the man who is patient under trial and stands up under temptation, for when he has stood the test and been approved, he will receive [the victor's] crown of life which God has promised to those who love Him." (James 1:12)

Don't Panic... It's Only a Test!

Have you ever been sitting at home in your most comfortable chair, watching your favorite television program, when suddenly, out of nowhere, a loud, beeping sound begins to clamor, a message flashes across your television screen and you hear... *"This is a test of the Emergency Broadcast System."* What thoughts run through your mind? Upon hearing the sound, do you immediately think the worst? Do you instantly go into defense mode, glare at your television set and wonder what is happening, or do you simply ignore the sounds, ignore the words, ignore the flashing lights, knowing within yourself this is only a test? *Take a moment and think about that...*

Our days are filled with mixed emotions - ups and downs, joys and pains, excitement and disappointment, anticipation and wonder, all vital ingredients that make up that four letter word... **LIFE!** But did you know that life will give you exactly what you give life? Life, with its many twists and turns, can trip you up, if you allow it. As crazy as it may sound, there are some events, some situations, some seemingly catastrophic moments that show up in your life that have the look and the feel of disaster. They will cause you to panic, lose it, and can even subtly push you to the edge and into a state of giving up. But I have some good news... **IT'S ONLY A TEST!**

To broadcast means to "transmit a program or some information openly."

A test of you what, you may say? It's only a test of <u>your</u> "emergency broadcast system." What will <u>you</u> broadcast when these events, situations and catastrophic moments knock at your door? What is your internal dialogue with yourself? What are you naming the test that you are facing? In an emergency who do you call for help? How do you broadcast what is happening in your life to your family, friends, coworkers, neighbors, church family, children?

"One's best success comes after their greatest disappointments." (Henry Ward Beecher)

In order for us to win in this game called life, we must be able to withstand *any* test, endure *any* trial, weather *any* storm and stand in the midst of the rain. When you are able to stand and not give up, when are you are able to persevere in the face of adversity, when you are able to hold your head up high even in the face of embarrassing moments, you increase your strength and fortitude to win and God gets the glory. Did you know that when you profess that God is your strength all eyes are on you? Believe it or not, people are watching you, but when they watch you they are really watching God. Isn't your God greater than any problem? Isn't your God greater than any situation? Isn't your God greater than any devil or enemy or bad report?

"Beloved, do not be amazed and bewildered at the fiery ordeal which is taking place to test your quality, as though something strange (unusual and alien to you and your position) were befalling you. But insofar as you are sharing Christ's sufferings, rejoice, so that when His glory [full of radiance and splendor] is revealed, you may also rejoice with triumph [exultantly]."
(1 Peter 4:12-13)

You can remain happy even when the facts are dictating that you should be panic. You can remain happy even when the facts are saying you should give up. You can remain happy even when the facts are saying you should throw in the towel. The question is whose report do you believe? Facts are never truth! Your bank account may be negative, but the truth of God says you are the "lender and not the borrower!" Whose report do you believe? Your body may be ailing and you may have received a negative diagnosis from the doctor, but the truth of God says, "By His stripes you are healed!" Whose report do you believe?

"The earth is the Lord's, and the fullness of it, the world and they who dwell in it." (Psalm 24:1)

It does not matter how bleak it looks in your natural, keep your eyes focused on the Truth of God. Direct your attention to the Spirit realm where God IS, and you will see that whatever challenge you face is only a test! Your ability to stand in the midst and proclaim, "I believe God's report," will make all the difference in the world. Why panic when your Heavenly Father already told you that He has everything under control? If He can create the universe and control all things therein, can He not rescue you from whatever you are going through? Everything belongs to Him, including you, and He protects everything that concerns Him.

REFRESHING KEY #27
Direct your attention to the Spirit realm where God IS!

Fight a Good Fight!

> *"Fight the good fight of faith, lay hold on eternal life,*
> *whereunto thou art also called, and hast professed a good*
> *profession before many witnesses."*
> (1 Timothy 6:12)

If we are going to fight, we must to fight the good fight of faith. Don't go around fighting all of the other stuff that is meaningless to you. If you are going to fight, fight the good fight of faith, because you will come out victorious. Regardless of what is happening in your natural world, God himself is in control of your life. Is there anything too hard for God? What situations, predicaments or conditions can we find ourselves in that God looks and says, "Not even I can help you out of that?" Could there ever be such a thing?

God himself can always reach down and work out the very things that seem impossible. He can work it out because He is sovereign (Psalm 115:3), because God does not lie (Number 23:19) and because all the promises of God in Him are yea and amen (2 Corinthians 1:20). God can do anything.

> *"There hath no temptation taken you but such as is common to*
> *man: but God is faithful, who will not suffer you to be tempted*
> *above that ye are able; but will with the temptation also make a*
> *way to escape, that ye may be able to bear it."*
> (1 Corinthians 10:13)

We have to be careful in this hour that we do not panic in situations that God has already made a way of escape. He has already made some promises to you, but because you allow your boat to be rocked out of control, because you allow the winds to overtake you, because you allow the seas to wreak havoc in your life, you fail to remember the very prophetic word or that vision that God gave you that assures you of your purpose and your destiny.

It reminds me of the disciples when they were on the on the boat with Jesus. (Mark 4:35-41) The winds came and the seas were raging and they started to panic. They asked Jesus an important question, *"Teacher, don't you care if we drown?"* (Mark 4:38) Aren't you concerned that we will die? The disciples were on the boat with the Master of the seas, the Master of the universe, but they lost sight not of who Christ was, but of who they were. They forgot the prophetic word that was spoken over their lives. They lost sight of the purpose for which they were walking with Christ in that hour.

REFRESHING KEY #28
Don't panic when Jesus is in your boat!

Many believers are in that same predicament today. They have lost sight of that which God has spoken in their lives, face challenging storms and are asking the Master, the One who has everything in control, "Don't you care about me?" They panic in the midst of pain and often feel like they have been blindsided when faced with devastating situations, even though Jesus has been in their "boat" the whole time. Jesus is there the whole time, yet they panic. Panic has the tendency to invade your emotions and ease your faith in God out of the equation. Your faith should proclaim God has everything in control. Don't panic when Jesus is in your boat calm and asleep.

Is there anything too hard for God? Have you ever found yourself in a situation where you believed not even God himself could rescue you? There are many who can confess that before they encountered the truth of God for themselves, they found themselves in situations from their past life before Christ, where even when they called on His name for help they did not believe that God would answer. However, even in the midst of us not knowing him He still reached out his loving hands and guided us, molded us and positioned us to move into purpose and destiny and awaken to who He is in our lives.

Everyone encounters storms in their lives. However, your level of faith can be gauged by what you do in the storm. It is difficult to gauge your true level of faith when the conditions around you are perfect, the sun is shining, the birds are chirping. But when the storms come, the winds rage, the clouds begin to thicken overhead and it begins to get dark, you immediately look for help. When you feel like you are losing control and feeling weak, that is the time to gauge your true level of faith, for His strength is made perfect in your weakness. (2 Corinthians 12:9) Do you really believe God? Do you really trust Him? Do you really believe that His word is true?

As a believer you have to ask yourself, where am I really in my faith? You can quote the Bible backwards and forwards, you give all of the "churchy" responses at the right time, but you may not trust God. You can seemingly have the form of godliness, but you lack the power thereof. (2 Timothy 3:5) The storms of life separate the men from the boys, the women from the girls. You have your hand in the Master's hand when the storms rise, the winds blow, the situations of life invade your territory at rapid speed, but you do not panic and give up. Everyone has human moments at points in their lives and may panic or become anxious or nervous. However, the human moments should only last for a moment. You must refuse to stay in those negative emotions, rise above them and tap into your faith in God.

REFRESHING KEY #29
Refuse to stay in negative emotions; rise above them and tap into your faith in God!

Jesus was in the boat with the disciples when they encountered the storm, panicked and awakened Him. Although Jesus spoke to the storm, rebuked the winds, and called everything to be at peace, He still had to separate himself from the disciples and go back down to the stern of the boat. He refused to allow the disciples to pull him into their consciousness. Jesus had to remain at the level that He was. He had to continue to trust God. He could not look at the storm and panic, as the disciples did. He knew that his Father had everything under control. He distinguished himself by speaking to the storm, the winds and the waves. He declared peace in the midst of chaos. He declared peace in the midst of the raging. He declared peace in the midst of the shaking.

"Do not be anxious about anything, but in every situation, by prayer and petition, with thanksgiving, present your requests to

*God. And the peace of God, which transcends all understanding,
will guard your hearts and your minds in Christ Jesus."*
(Philippians 4:6-7)

Peace is the antidote to panic. Peace is defined as "freedom from disturbance; quiet; tranquility." In the midst of the storm, Jesus declared quiet and tranquility. This peace surpassed all human understanding. The declaration of peace is the antidote to chaotic, stormy, disturbing, tumultuous experiences in life. Declare peace when it feels like everything around you is crumbling. Declare peace when you receive a negative report. Declare peace when your relationships seem to take a turn for the worst. Separate yourself from wrong thinking, distorted imagery, negative ideologies and limiting belief systems. Recognize God in the midst of thee.

Jesus was in the stern of the boat while the disciples were watching the winds rage, yet Jesus did not panic. He retreated to a place and went to sleep. I would think that the smartest thing to do would be to go where Jesus is. But their human side began to take over. Their emotions began to gain control over Spirit. They focused on the storm instead of focusing on the Master of the storm.

REFRESHING KEY #30
Look for the rainbow instead of the rage!

Oftentimes, in the midst of calamity we want to see what is coming, and as we watch the situation worsening panic ensues. The more you focus on the problem, the more the problem appears to worsen and everything you see is magnified. But if you were able to retreat to where God is, to where God says it is safe, to where God says there is peace, you can stand in the storm. You can look for the rainbow instead of the rage. You can rest in faith and not fear and see God causing you to triumph in every situation.

Speak to It!

"Death and life are in the power of the tongue: and they that love it shall eat the fruit thereof." (Proverbs 18:21)

The Bible says that life and death are in the power of the tongue. Your words carry either life or death. Your words matter. You have the power to speak death to the storm and it will die, the same as you have the power to speak life to the storm and it will live. It is your choice. Jesus spoke peace to the storm and the storm ceased. If you know you are doing the will of the Father, then whenever you encounter a storm you have to remind yourself that you are safe and protected. *(Side Note: This is conditional. If you are not doing the Father's will, God may send a storm into your life to get your attention. Once you get into His will the storm will cease.)*

When you know that you are in the will of God and see the storms begin to rage in your life, you must command the storm to be still. You can look in the face of adversity and command it to settle. Speak to your emotions and say, *"Listen, emotions, we are not going to get out of control today. We are staying calm."* You have to keep speaking to that storm, 24 hours a day, 7 days a week, every second of the day. As the storm is raging you have to remind yourself, "Self, we are not going to lose our mind."

REFRESHING KEY #31
Your words carry either life or death!

David said, *"I would have fainted unless I believed to see the goodness of the Lord in the land of the living."* (Psalm 27:13) You have to desire to see the goodness of the Lord in the land of the living, in this life. Don't give up because the storm is raging, because if the truth be told, after that storm ceases another one will come at some point in life. You may not know the hour or the day, but another storm will come. God will periodically send storms in our lives to challenge us, to check us and to continually gauge our faith level. Don't die <u>in</u> the storm. Survive and thrive <u>through</u> the storm.

Instead of going where Jesus was and partaking of what He was doing, the disciples decided to focus on the storm, the external circumstances, the conditions of nature. They were bewildered that Jesus was calm. They were confused about how He could sleep in the midst of the storm. Was He really asleep or could He have been meditating in the midst of what was going on, thanking God for victory and safety? Stop focusing on the negativity that is around you and place your focus on the Christ that is living on the inside of you.

The Bible says we are to *"set our affection on things above, not on things on the earth."* (Colossians 3:2) Focus your attention on God, not your situation. Focus your attention within, not without. I believe that if the disciples had the same God-consciousness as Jesus, then they too could have also spoken to the seas and to the winds. This was a teachable moment. Jesus was in the same boat as the disciples. The entire boat was experiencing the storm. Yet, He was able to rest in the stern of the boat while the storm was raging, because He knew that his Heavenly Father had everything under control. The disciples panicked as they watched the storm raging from the top of the boat and felt powerless. As a result, Jesus had to show the manifestation and the power of God through the storm. Your storms are the time for God's glory to be made manifest in your life for the world to see. It is the appointed time to speak the word of God so that God can be glorified.

REFRESHING KEY #32
Your storms are the time for God's glory to be made manifest in your life for the world to see!

You have three options in the storm. You can either 1) completely give up and die in the storm; 2) rest in God and know that He is working everything together for your good; or 3) put on your "bold clothes" and speak to the storm. If you choose not to retreat to where God is, the place where you can to rest in the storm, but you choose to stand on top of the ship and watch the winds blowing, the seas raging, the boat rocking back and forth and the devastation that is coming in your direction, then you have to be bold enough to speak to that storm!

Many of people have curious minds. They do not like anticipation. They want to see what is coming, even though they know that it could devastate them and overtake them. If you are bold enough to watch the storm raging, then you better be bold enough to speak to it! Know the right language to speak to the storm so that it will not overtake you and your family. Speak words that will calm the raging storm. Speak words that will slow the winds and calm the seas. Why? God said that we could and everything that God is we are.

Can You Hear Him?

"And after the earthquake a fire; but the LORD was not in the fire: and after the fire a still small voice. And it was so, when Elijah heard it, that he wrapped his face in his mantle, and went out, and stood in the entering in of the cave. And, behold, there came a voice unto him, and said, What doest thou here, Elijah?"
(1 Kings 19:12-13)

You have to be solid in what the Father is saying, even in the midst of the storm. You have to tune your ear into what God is saying, because in the storm it can get pretty loud. You have to be able to tap in to hear God's still, small voice speaking in the midst of the chaos. In order for you to triumph in the storm, in order for you to purpose in your heart that you will not die in the process, you have to not only effectively speak to the storm, not only get yourself to where God is, but you have to make sure that you are surrounded by the right people. If you are surrounded by doubters, those who do not believe the God on the inside of you, you will assume that the storm was designed to overtake you. You will assume that the storm was a punishment for your wrongdoing.

Therefore, you must be able to hear God. Kick the negative voices out of your experience. Focus on Him. Keep your eyes on God, not on the storm. Keep your ears in tune with His voice, not the haters, the doubters, the fearful. Go to the place where God is and sit in the rest of God. If you are facing a situation right now, if you are in the midst of a trial, stop where you are and repeat… **"This is only a test…for God is my Source!"** Repeat this affirmation every day until you feel the breakthrough within you. Then repeat it every day thereafter until you see the manifested promises of God come to full fruition in your life. I promise you God will never lie to you!

IF HE SAID IT, BELIEVE IT…AND THAT SETTLES IT!

Chapter Six
YOU'RE BIGGER THAN THAT!

"...greater is He that is in you, than he that is in the world."

(1 John 4:4)

The Journey

- Do you find yourself sweating the small stuff?
- Have you allowed others to stop you from believing in the promises of God for your life?
- Have you decided to give up?

Michael was a powerful communicator. His words attracted people. Whenever Michael spoke, people would listen. No matter what was going on, when Michael entered a room, all focus was on him. He always had this trait, even as a young child. In school, Michael held many leadership positions (captain of the football team, class president). Even in kindergarten, Michael was often selected to be the line leader.

Throughout college and his adult life, Michael used his voice for change. He was an advocate for the community and for justice. He always spoke up for what he felt was right. He was always speaking on behalf of those who had no voice. Michael would often lead rallies and protests for justice. But there was one problem, Michael was able to fight for the rights of others, but he was not able to fight for himself. He always found himself the victim of racial injustice and discrimination. Michael graduated from college with a degree in journalism, yet he was unable to break into the field. No matter how many doors he knocked on, no one gave him a chance.

After over 10 years of trying to break into the journalism field, Michael gave up. Although he enjoyed fighting on behalf of others, he became very discouraged with his own life. He became so discouraged that he put many of his life goals and dreams on the shelf, settling for where he was in life and concluding that he had to always fight for others, a passion that he had, but never gaining real monetary reward or personal success.

You have to purpose in your life to never give up!

Michael had given up. He had accepted the lie of someone else and did not accept the truth of who God created him to be. He allowed himself to be oppressed by the opinions and thoughts of others, allowed others to stop him from dreaming and ultimately, became discouraged.

One day, Michael was on his way to a rally and stopped for a cup of coffee. In the coffee shop was one of the city officials. Michael began to strike up a conversation and found that they had a lot in common. Michael began to share his views and even opened up about his goals and dreams that he had put on the shelf and explained how no one would give him a break into the field of his dreams.

Michael had lost his edge. He lost his ability to dream. He lost his ability to create a path for himself. In this journey called life, sometimes you just have to break the cycle of allowing yourself to be oppressed by the thoughts of others. Most of our failures in life come from walking away from what we know to do. All of us have had situations where we knew what to do, but we just didn't do it. But in this hour, God is bringing back to our remembrance the original plan that He had for us before the foundation of the world.

GOD'S ORIGINAL PLAN WAS FOR YOU TO HAVE DOMINION OVER THE EARTH!

Michael was ready for change. He was ready to go back to God's original plan for his life. Michael got his mind back! He went on a "change journey" and for 60 days, Michael focused on who God created him to be. After the 60 days, Michael began to apply for journalist positions. He even knocked on doors that were once closed in his face, and much to Michael's surprise he found a position at a top news station. Today, he serves as a news anchor and has his own investigative reporting program. His voice is now heard around the world, being a voice for the voiceless, creating change for others, while at the same time prospering in every area of his life!

Your Appointed Time

"Is anything too hard for the Lord? At the appointed time I will return unto thee according to the time of life and Sarah shall have a son." (Genesis 18:14)

God promised Abraham that he and Sarah would conceive a son at an appointed time, a year from when he spoke it. To Abraham and Sarah that time seemed to be afar off. Yet God had an appointed time, a set time, a designated time. God continually speaks to us concerning our future. He has an appointed time set for each and every level of our destiny. Every day we see the unfolding of His promise. Every day we pass another test. Every day we encounter the storms of life at some level. Every day our boats are being rocked. Every day the winds are blowing and the seas are raging. However, if you shift your focus from your circumstance to the prophetic word that God has spoken over your life, you will see God unfolding His plan.

Knowing that there is an appointed time for God's word to manifest in your life should cause you to live in expectation. When you live in expectation you anticipate God's manifestation at any moment of the day. You are in expectation until your due season manifests. You are in expectation even in the midst of adversity, because you know you are in your due season. It is in this realm that you experience the joy of the Lord, your strength to endure any trial, hardship, adversity or challenge.

REFRESHING KEY #33
Stay in God-expectation, even through adversity!

The joy of the Lord is experienced at the place of expectation. You cannot experience the joy of the Lord if you focus on the things in your physical surrounding that could cause you to doubt the promise that God has spoken in your life. We have to be able to tap into the place of expectation so that we have joy for a season that is up and coming.

God will often promise you something that seems impossible in your natural experience. The Bible says that Sarah laughed within herself when God promised that she would conceive a son even though she was beyond childbearing age. Sarah considered her physical body and thought the promise was impossible. She laughed when she heard the promise from God.

But when God asked her if she laughed, she immediately denied it. Sometimes God will make us a promise, but the situations around us can be so dreadful that it is difficult to believe God. When doubt consumes your mind God can send positive thought to cancel it out. As soon as Sarah laughed, as soon as she started to deny or refuse the prophetic word, another thought came in and refuted it.

When God begins to manifest His promises in your life, he will stir up conditions around you that will make you laugh at the prophecy that he gave you and cause you to believe that is impossible. But if you stay in the season of expectation and maintain the posture of expectation, then no matter what factors arise to cause you to doubt, they will not stop you from doing the thing that God has asked you to do. As a matter of fact, the negative occurrences should be fuel for you to keep moving forward. Keep your eyes focused on your appointed season, the due season that is yet coming your way.

REFRESHING KEY #34
The rainbow is an indication that the storm is over!

A rainbow often appears after a rain storm. The rainbow is an indication that the storm is over. In life, you have to anticipate seeing the rainbow. Why? Because God said it. This time next year, at the appointed season, you will reap if you faint not. In your due season if you don't give up, if you don't get weary in your well doing, if you don't get tired of believing in Him, though you will have to fight your way through the adversity, adversity that will cause people to question why you believe God, you will reap the harvest. You will not doubt God. You will not waver in your faith.

It is difficult being on God's side because you have to be in expectation of that which you cannot see any natural signs of manifesting. Oftentimes, the storms of life do not have any natural, visible signs of their dissent in your life. You don't see the illness coming. You don't see the divorce coming. You don't see losing your house or losing your car. You don't see your children going wayward. These are things that you don't see coming. But in the midst of all hell breaking loose, there is a promise that God has made and there is a season for its manifestation. For every negative thought, God sends an angel our way to cancel it out.

If you stay in the realm of expectation, you will be able to ignore your naysayers. Naysayers gravitate to those who seek to remain in the presence of God and live their lives according to His purpose. Every time you try to push toward destiny and manifest God's greatness in your life, naysayers seem to line up at your door. They ring your phone off the hook. They knock on your door constantly. Your naysayers will say, *"Are you really sure God called you to do that? It does not look like it is working. If I were you I would fold it up." "You don't have the money for that school." "They are no longer giving aid for that venture. Do you see the economy?"*

They feed you their negative garbage and by the time you leave their presence you have begun to question God. *"Am I called?" "Am I supposed to do this?" "Will the provision ever come?" "Will the thing that God promised me come to pass?" "Am I in the right place?"*

You begin to question everything the Lord told you because you were in the company of the naysayers. However, if you can ignore your naysayers and live in expectation of your appointed season, your due season, then you can stand on top of the boat, look at the storm and speak - *"Storm, I am looking above you. I am looking over you. I see the rainbow!"*

REFRESHING KEY #35
If you stay in the realm of expectation, you will be able to ignore your naysayers!

There is a prophetic word that will walk you through situations at a slow pace. It will walk you through the different seasons of your life, through the roadblocks, challenges and pitfalls that were in your childhood, teen years and adult life. But there is also a prophetic word that cuts through the roadblocks, mental challenges, pitfalls and catastrophes of your life and gets right to the core of the situation, the root of the problem. It gets to the heart of the matter.

The prophetic word can walk you through seasons and at the same time it can get to the core of a situation, because God knows what you need to hear at your appointed time and season. God will speak through those who are sensitive to the Holy Spirit, those who do not want to abuse the people, but heal the people, those who do not want to manipulate the people, but help them, those who do not use their prophetic gift for their own selfish reasons, but for the building and edification of the kingdom of God.

God speaks to you wherever you are at the moment, but he does not speak to your condition. God speaks to your future self. God speaks to your potential. God speaks to the one He created. But you have to trust God and His prophets. You may be going through a difficult season in your life, but God does not see your difficulty. God sees you victorious. God sees you free. God speaks to the one He created, the original you, not the one who developed as a result of life issues.

God's ways are always greater. God's vision for your life is always perfect, because He sees you as the creation that He created. As you progress in life, God gives you clarity on what He created you to do. Therefore, whatever challenges you face, they are only temporary. It's a fleeting, passing moment. God's vision for you is so much greater.

"For our light affliction, which is but for a moment, worketh for us a far more exceeding and eternal weight of glory; While we look not at the things which are seen, but at the things which are not seen: for the things which are seen are temporal; but the things which are not seen are eternal." (2 Corinthians 4:17-18)

Do You See What God Sees?

"But Jesus beheld them, and said unto them, With men this is impossible; but with God all things are possible."
(Matthew 19:26)

God has instilled in us His greater purpose and has empowered us with the gift of expectation that allows us to take our eyes off of what is happening in our natural experience (the seen) and focus on what God is doing in the Spirit (the unseen). If you allow yourself to focus solely on your natural experience and the situations that are happening around you, then you will doubt what God has spoken in your life and attempt to change God's mind concerning His purpose and plan for your life. You will try to convince Him that it will not come to pass.

Many people try to talk God out of His plan and purpose for their lives, and as a result, they go through life confused, frustrated, fearful, intimidated, lacking the motivation to attain greatness. *"God, do you really mean me? Are you sure I'm the one? Maybe you did not notice that I do not have all of the money that I need to accomplish what you are asking me to do." "I lack the educational credentials that I need. I don't see how it is possible."*

REFRESHING KEY #36
God uses people to prove His existence!

However, we serve a God who is magnified in the face of impossibility. He does his best work when the situation looks impossible. God performs his greatest miracles in the midst of impossibility so that people (onlookers, friends, family, neighbors, coworkers, haters, naysayers, doubters and strangers) can look at your life and witness that God does exist. God uses people to prove His existence. He will reveal himself in the midst of your struggle and launch you into a wealthy place just to prove to others that He is God. The question is do you trust Him? Do you see what God sees? You have to be able to see yourself as God sees you.

You may be in a storm right now as you are reading this book, but instead of panicking and questioning whether God is concerned that you may perish, focus your attention on what God has sent you to the earth to accomplish. Focus your attention on fulfilling your assignment. Instead of thinking about your situation, think on the things that are right and just and pure and noteworthy of praise. Don't think on the calamity and the devastation, think on purpose, destiny, manifestation.

"Finally, brethren, whatsoever things are true, whatsoever things are honest, whatsoever things are just, whatsoever things are pure, whatsoever things are lovely, whatsoever things are of good report; if there be any virtue, and if there be any praise, think on these things." (Philippians 4:8)

When the storm was raging Jesus first calmed the storm, then He gave the disciples the "red tape" prophetic word. He asked them a very poignant question, "Why are you so fearful? How is it that you have no faith?" (Mark 4:40) Jesus halted the conditions that were happening around them so that they could focus their attention on the real issue - fear. God will stop everything to get your attention, but many believers can get confused. They panic in the storm, pray for the Father's help, and when the storm ceases they say, "The Father must have heard my prayer." But God could be saying, "Let me stop this storm for a minute so I can get your attention, because you are about to spin out of control." Then once He gets your attention he stirs things up again to watch your reaction. Are you going to exercise faith or fear? Are you going to trust Him or doubt Him? You were not designed to live in panic. You were designed to trust God.

The storm is designed to make you better, not bitter. Jesus said in this life you are going to have tribulations and trials and situations and calamity. (John 16:33) It's a promise. You are going to go through those things, but in the end you will win. In the end you are the victor, not the victim. You emerge as the champion. That means that you must always be forward looking, forward thinking. You have to be able to lift yourself up and see beyond the storm. You have to be able to see the rainbow breaking through the clouds. Why? It is an indication that the storm is over.

REFRESHING KEY #37
If God made you a promise, you have to believe it!

If God made you a promise, you have to believe it. If God has spoken his word over your life, but your natural conditions do not align with what He has spoken to you in Spirit, then you have trust God. He always keeps his promise. On the road to greatness you will encounter contrary winds, but know that if it is contrary, it is only temporary. How you come out of the storm is dependent on how you go through the storm. In the midst of the storm no matter how cloudy it is, no matter how dark it may seem, you must see what God sees.

Speak peace where there is panic. Speak life where there is death. Speak victory where it looks like defeat. Instead of saying, *"This is overwhelming; this is causing me to panic; this is making me fearful; this is making me upset; I am going to give up,"* remind yourself of who God created you to be. Instead of giving your attention to the situation, give your attention to God. That is the fight. Yes, it is easier said than done. Our human side tries to go to battle and we begin to speak words of panic. It is in those times that you have to fight the good fight of faith. (1 Timothy 6:12) Remind yourself that you are the head and not the tail. Remind yourself that you are above only and not beneath. Remind yourself that God made you the lender, not the borrower. No matter what you go through, see yourself winning.

Don't Run... Rest!

One word of caution... Do not choose to sleep in the storm and deaden yourself to the pain that is going on in your life. Some people call themselves being calm in the storm and revert to a vice (drugs, alcohol, sex) to dull their senses to what is happening in their natural surroundings and cause them to escape from what is happening. God does not want you to escape. He wants you to rest in Him.

There is a powerful prayer written by Reinhold Niebuhr that says, *"God grant me the serenity to accept the things I cannot change, the courage to change the things that I can, and the wisdom to know the difference."* This is what you speak to your storm. We have to be able to accept the things that we cannot change, because sometimes the storm is not going to change right away. You have to be able to accept it and move through it, because it is only coming to pass. But the things that we can change we have to ask God for the grace in the midst of the storm to be able to change those things. We have to be able to identify those things that are causing us to be fearful. We have to be honest with ourselves so that we can have the breakthrough and the deliverance that we need.

REFRESHING KEY #38
No matter what it looks like, rest in Him!

After Sarah laughed concerning the promise that God made to her and the angels reminded her that she laughed, she did not say, "Well, I don't believe it anyway." She had to cancel out the negative thought that the blessing could not come to pass. God will allow us to go through situations to expose and dispel the negativity in our lives so that when negative thoughts come we can cancel them and move towards our purpose and our destiny. The disciples were fearful and afraid when the storm began to rage, but at least they had the common sense to go down to where the help was (to where Jesus was in the ship sleeping), because if they had stayed at the top of the boat and watched the storm they would have died in their own fear.

As we discussed, Sarah laughed at the promise. She laughed at the prophetic word that she heard. Did she laugh because she really didn't believe the promise or did she laugh because it was so crazy that she knew everybody else would not believe it? Oftentimes, we will laugh at the promise or feel like it is impossible to come to pass because we feel like others will not believe it. Sometimes you laugh to brace yourself for any impending disappointment, yet you really hope that it will come to pass.

God may give you a promise or reveal to you what you will manifest in this life, but your present surroundings causes it to appear impossible to manifest, and those around you (family and friends) do not believe it either. You may share a part of what God has shown you and they look at you in disbelief, and just so you

101

don't look like a fool you will laugh with them and then retreat by yourself and say, *"God, please bring it to pass."* You are fearful to show your faith in God because it looks unbelievable in the natural. You don't want to show that you believe God at his word, because you want to be accepted by others. You don't want to be the laughing stock, the brunt of the jokes, so you laugh with them. You pretend that you don't believe what God said, but in your heart you are hoping that His word will manifest.

REFRESHING KEY #39
When God makes us a promise he will bring it to pass!

It takes a bold person to trust and believe God. If God says you are going to be the greatest real estate tycoon the world has ever seen, yet in your natural experience you lost everything and you have nothing tangible to manifest that word, it takes a bold person to say, this is only temporary. It takes a bold person to proclaim that you believe in the word from God that you cannot see in your natural, but you know in your heart is real. Marianne Williamson said it best - "Our biggest fear is not that we are inadequate. Our deepest fear is that we are powerful beyond measure." So, what are you really afraid of? You are afraid of the fact that you are powerful beyond measure, that you can really come out of your situation if you can survive the storm within your own mind and only see what God sees.

When God makes us a promise he is going to bring it to pass. He made a promise to Abraham that he would make him the father of many nations. When God makes us a promise he doesn't make a promise just for the sake making a promise. He makes it as a decree to show how mighty and how powerful he can move in and through our lives.

He Calls the Shots

"And he goeth up into a mountain, and calleth unto him whom he would: and they came unto him. And he ordained twelve, that they should be with him, and that he might send them forth to preach, And to have power to heal sicknesses, and to cast out devils:" (Mark 3:13-15)

Mark 3:13-15, lets us know that God will call us into that which He desires for us to do in the earth. You will go through storms, you will go through trials, tests and situations, but you have to fight to remember the reason why you are here. You have to remember the purpose that God has spoken over your life. There was no way the disciples could perish on that boat because God had already called them and anointed them to heal the sick and cast out demons in the earth. He already had a plan for their lives. He already predestined them to do great things. He already had a plan for them, but they forgot. The world is full of those who have forgotten that Christ has called them to himself and He has set them aside for a time such as this. At the right season and at the right moment He will reveal who you are to the world.

REFRESHING KEY #40
God is not like man!

God is not like man. If God calls you to something, he already has the plan in place of how you will accomplish it. If man calls you to do something, he can change his mind and stop you at any moment that he chooses. He can sideline you at his will. One day you're leading the team to victory, and the next day you're sitting on the bench unaware of the reason that you were sidelined. But when God calls you he doesn't call you to sideline you. Man can be wishy-washy. He can be on today and off tomorrow. But when you tap into the purpose of God for your life and stay in His will, you will never be sidelined.

The conditions in your natural may dictate to the outside world that you have been sidelined, but because you know God and you understand His voice, you know that what you're going through is temporary. The storm cannot sideline you. Sickness cannot sideline you. Loss of employment cannot sideline you. You must declare in your heart, *"This storm must be God trying to speak to me. It must be God trying to elevate me to another level. It must be God trying to stir up my faith a little more."* God has a bigger plan. Just keep your eyes on the big picture.

God calls us to greatness. His calling does not negate the storms that are coming, but it is designed to keep us working the gift of God that is on the inside of us - His purpose, His plan, His destiny for our lives. If you are going through a storm right now, know that you are you are going to get some relief. If you are not going through a storm, know that some storms will come. It is not designed for you to be afraid. It is designed for you to be equipped. If you learn how to be equipped to go through your storm, as you meet others who are going through a storm you are able to help them get to the place where they don't panic and give up.

REFRESHING KEY #41
Don't panic in the storm!

Before Oprah Winfrey manifested her true greatness to the world, she had to go through some storms. She had to go through some impossible moments. She had to endure some trials that would cause the average person to die in the process. Those who tried to evaluate her life based on her trials and rendered her useless were greatly disappointed years later. Many people may not have looked at what God was doing beyond the storm. There were some who did and they helped push her to her destiny. But others tried to keep her in a lowly place, a desolate place, a depressed place.

When you are in the company of those who are going through a storm, when you walk into the midst of those who are dealing with devastating situations what do you say? Do you allow them to just sit in their storm and panic? Do you rock with them, sway with them and panic with them?

"That we henceforth be no more children, tossed to and fro, and carried about with every wind of doctrine, by the sleight of men, and cunning craftiness, whereby they lie in wait to deceive; But speaking the truth in love, may grow up into him in all things, which is the head, even Christ:" (Ephesians 4:14-15)

Your ability to help others see beyond their storm will strengthen your ability to see beyond your own storms. But you have to grow up in God. You have to grow up into Him. You have to grow up into knowing who God is. Because you are human you may faint for a moment in the midst of your storm. You may find yourself getting overwhelmed. But it should only last for a minute, because in the twinkling of an eye God can change the entire situation. In the twinkling of an eye God can change the entire picture. In the twinkling of an eye the storm started to rage. One minute everything was great. The next minute it seemed like all hell had broken loose. Well, it also works in the reverse. If you are in the midst of storm, God can cause it to cease immediately.

REFRESHING KEY #42
Know your appointed season!

Therefore, be settled in the storm. Be at peace in the storm. Remind yourself of your purpose in the storm. Know your appointed season. Know the season that you are in. There are some things that God has spoken over your life that are supposed to come to pass at a particular time in your life, but you have to recognize your season. You have to remember the prophetic word that was spoken over your life. You have to remember the vision, the dream, the thought that God placed on the inside of you. You have to fight through the negativity. You have to fight through the craziness that is going on inside of your mind. You have to draw on one nugget that is going to place you on the road to purpose and land you in the future of destiny.

You have to speak to the storm. What do we say? You have to craft your language. You have to say what God is saying. Don't douse the fire. God is working on the outside and he is working on the inside. He is bringing his plan together. Your appointed season, your due season is just over the horizon if you don't give up. What do you say in the storm? *"I was born to manifest the glory of God that is within me!"* You have to be determined. You have to be focused. When your emotions begin to overtake you and you begin to feel like you are going in the wrong direction, make sure that your voice can carry.

God is working miracles in this hour. You are living in the appointed time for your purpose to take legs and begin to walk. There are things that God has spoken over our lives and now we are living in that appointed time of manifestation. But in order for us to get where we have to go, there are certain things that God has designed for us to go through. There are certain challenges that we must meet just because we are here on the earth, just because we are proclaiming who God is and the greatness of God.

If you are feeling faint, you better run to the person who knows the voice of God for your life, someone who can pull you up out of that state. The wrong voices will cause you to give up. The wrong voices will cause you to drown in the face of your deep. We have all had wrong people in our lives that could have caused us to die in the midst of our storms. But you have to pray that God will bring the right people in your life to help you understand the might and the power of God and realize that nothing can stand in your way. This is the season for you to go after it. Whatever you want in life you have to go after it. Remove all of the fear, remove all of the doubt. Go after it. Why? Because you are bigger than that!

BIG THINGS OFTEN COME IN SMALL PACKAGES!

If you allow the thoughts and opinions of negative people to cloud your vision, you will walk further and further away from who God has called you to be and what God created you to do. Never let negative people cloud your focus and get you off track. Isn't it amazing that this great, big, loving God deposited

His purpose and His plan into your small human frame! That is why you can boldly proclaim... **"I'm Bigger than that!"**

"For we are his workmanship, created in Christ Jesus unto good works, which God hath before ordained that we should walk in them." (Ephesians 2:10)

Serenity Prayer

God grant me the serenity
to accept the things I cannot change;
courage to change the things I can;
and wisdom to know the difference.

Living one day at a time;
enjoying one moment at a time;
accepting hardships as the pathway to peace;
taking, as He did, this sinful world
as it is, not as I would have it;
trusting that He will make all things right
if I surrender to His Will;
that I may be reasonably happy in this life
and supremely happy with Him
forever in the next.
Amen.

Chapter Seven
CAST YOUR CARES

"Humble yourselves therefore under the mighty hand of God, that he may exalt you in due time: Casting all your care upon him; for he careth for you." (1 Peter 5:6-7)

Revenge - The Stealer of Dreams

*M*aggie was a very well-liked and well-respected person among her peers. In school she was always voted, "Best Dressed," or "Most Likely to Succeed," or "Most Popular." Maggie was very bright and always seemed to excel at whatever project she embarked upon. These traits carried over to her adult life. Maggie was successful on her job, in her church, and in her community. She was asked to speak at many community functions and was often hailed as the example of a person who is able to accomplish whatever they set their mind and heart to do.

Maggie was a hair designer and owned a salon that was very successful. She had over 25 employees and prided herself on running a company that was very professional and whose number one focus was the quality service rendered to the customers. Maggie had a very high level clientele. Doctors, lawyers, business owners, city officials and entertainers visited Maggie's salon for their grooming needs on a daily basis. Maggie was at the top of her game.

One day, Maggie decided to expand her organization and hire three additional hair designers. Her goal was to open three new salons by the end of the year. Maggie trained the new employees and instilled in them her vision for the business. For three years, Maggie's business increased. Her referrals increased and her customers were happy. However, right in the midst of one of the best times of her life, one of Maggie's employees (Jennifer) started to change. Jennifer started to think that she could run the business better than Maggie. Jennifer began to slander Maggie's name to her customers and spread rumors and lies about Maggie's business practices. Suddenly, Maggie's business started to slow down. She began losing clients and her employees began to complain.

Maggie found out that Jennifer was the culprit who was spreading the lies about her and decided to fire Jennifer immediately. Jennifer, already prepared for the outcome, left the company and opened her own salon, bringing 50% of Maggie's clients with her. Maggie was very upset, hurt and disappointed. She prided herself on treating her employees well. She didn't understand why Jennifer would do this to her. Maggie became very angry and set out to get revenge. She wanted to make Jennifer feel as bad as she felt, if not worse. She wanted Jennifer's clients to know the real Jennifer. She wanted Jennifer's business to fail.

Maggie put all of her energy into retaliating against Jennifer and seeking revenge. It became her number one priority. She spent so many hours of her day trying to bring Jennifer down that she lost focus of her own business. Maggie, the once happy, jovial, well-liked, popular, easygoing person, was now bitter, angry, depressed and vengeful – a very bad combination for success.

Maggie's best friend, Erica, noticed the change in her and decided to take matters into her own hands. She suggested to Maggie that she needed to channel those negative feelings into positive energy and begin to let go of the weight of resentment and revenge. Erica explained to Maggie that the more she harbored the feelings of anger and resentment, the more she would remain imprisoned in her own mind and would feel in bondage to her own thoughts. Maggie was open and receptive to what she heard. All she wanted was to go back to the "Maggie" she once knew - the successful, happy, excited Maggie, the Maggie that could make things happen.

Maggie wanted to let go of her anger and get back on track with her success and with her destiny. Erica suggested that Maggie come with her to church and seek God for answers. Maggie agreed. For months they attended Sunday worship services, bible studies, prayer meetings, conferences so Maggie could hear from God. Maggie even sought the face of God in in own time, gaining command of her prayer life and committing herself wholeheartedly to Him. She was amazed. Her thoughts began to change and she began to let go of the anger and allow God to take care of the rest. She sought peace within herself and resisted the temptation to allow her mind to dwell on the negative.

After six months Maggie's life changed. She let go of her anger and allowed her fears to subside. She was no longer concerned about what Jennifer was doing or how Jennifer was living her life. Maggie focused on the God within herself and found power to overcome the negativity that Jennifer had tossed in her direction. She was able to cast her cares on the Father and he truly showed his favor in her life.

Today, Maggie owns not only three salons, but she has expanded to open four full-service salons in three major cities. She attributes all glory to God who turned her life around and directed her off the road of destruction and back onto the road to destiny.

Revenge is defined as "the desire to take vengeance or retaliate." Revenge is a very strong desire. It is a desire that can cause hurt, harm or danger to a person, but more so, it is a desire that destroys the person harboring the desire in his/her heart. Oftentimes, when a person is determined to get revenge for a wrong to which they were subjected, they unknowingly put themselves in bondage and inflict undue punishment on themselves.

Unconditional Love

- Did you know that the Father truly care for you?
- Did you know that you can bring your cares to Him and He will heal your hurt?
- Did you know that there is nothing that you can do that will cause the Father to reject you?

There are those who need to hear that God cares. There are those who need to hear that the Father is there for them. There are those who need to hear that God has not forgotten them. You can bring your problems to the Father. You can bring any and every situation to the Father. There is nothing that you can bring to the

Father that will cause Him to reject you or refuse to stretch out his loving hand to you if you come to him with a pure heart and are focused on being the best you. I cannot think of any situation that anyone can face that, if they honestly in their heart and in their mind seek change, the Father will not answer.

You do not have to panic. You do not have to throw in the towel. You do not have to turn your back. You do not have to seek revenge. You do not have to retaliate. You don't have to try to sleep the day away. You don't have to get angry or frustrated. The scripture reminds us that we can cast our cares upon Him because He cares for us. Our Heavenly Father cares for you.

There are people who are unsure of God's love. Some are unsure and some are unaware of what God is capable of doing in their lives. There are those who, right now, are throwing in the towel and giving up because the situations of life have t beat them down, all because they do not know who they are and they do not know their Creator.

"And be not conformed to this world: but be ye transformed by the renewing of your mind, that ye may prove what is that good, and acceptable, and perfect, will of God." (Romans 12:2)

We are living in a world that has fallen and only the saints of God, those that have been strengthened by the Holy Ghost realize that we can lift people's consciousness, lift people's minds and point the people back to the Father. There are those who have taken God at His word and has purposed in their hearts to live this life God's way. They boldly proclaim the goodness of God. They do not allow their faith to be shaken by outward circumstances.

They refuse to let the world beat them down. They will not allow the world to have the final say in their lives. They claim victory through Christ.

REFRESHING KEY #43
Take your problems to God, the One who has the power to change your situation!

We must believe and know by faith that the God we serve, the God that we believe in, the God that we know, the God that we love is a healer, a deliver, a mind restorer and a heart repairer. If you want to succeed in life and achieve the outcome that you desire, then you must stop taking your problems to those who are unable to give you the solutions. Take your problems to God, the One who has the power to change your situation. Stop taking your problems to those who enjoy watching you live in a continual pity party. Seek the company of those who are not comfortable with the state that you are in and are so connected with the Father that they are compelled to speak words of life to you that will help change your situation. Their advice may seem offensive at first, yet it is the very thing that you need to hear that will cause you to run back to the Father and seek His face.

When you cast your cares on Him, you have to really cast them. If you cast your worries on God, if you allow Him to do what He promised he would do in your life and you concentrate on doing the thing that He sent you here to do, you will experience the hand of God moving mightily in your life. If you want to experience the breakthroughs, the miracles, the peace of God that passes all understanding, you have to be able to let go of whatever is holding you bound - hurt, depression, sin, disappointment, rejection, revenge, retaliation. You have to let go and let God.

REFRESHING KEY #44
When we cast our cares on God we get His attention!

Many Christians say they let go and let God, but in their hearts they are still holding on to strongholds. They are still dwelling in the emotion of the problem, worrying, trying to figure out the outcome by natural means and trying to make it all work. However, you cannot solve a problem that requires a supernatural answer with natural means. It is impossible. I believe that it is crucial for us to do what the Father says, cast all of our cares on Him. When we are able to do that, then we can eliminate some of the unnecessary stress that we put upon ourselves. The Father promised that He would not put more on us than we can bear. (1 Corinthians 10:13)

Acts 27:25 says, *"Wherefore, sirs, be of good cheer: for I believe God, that it shall be even as it was told me."* When you cast your cares upon the Father, when you bring your cares to the Him you are saying, *"I believe God. I believe the very thing that He has whispered in my ear. I believe the very thing that He has shown me in my dreams. I know that prayer changes things. I know that prayer gets the Father's attention on my behalf."* When we cast our cares on God we get His attention. It shows Him that we are humble and realize that the victory that we have is not because of who we are, but it is because we believe in the God who is continually whispering good things in our ear.

I Believe God

Every day you have to condition yourself to love God, to serve Him and do what He has called you to do. You have to remind yourself in the midst of whatever you are going through in the natural that you believe God. You have to believe God even when He has given you a dream that is bigger than what your resources may dictate. You have to believe God when he has given you an assignment that is bigger than your surroundings. You have to believe God when he has made you promises that do not appear in your natural like they will to come to pass.

"God is not a man, that he should lie; neither the son of man, that he should repent: hath he said, and shall he not do it? or hath he spoken, and shall he not make it good?" (Number 23:19)

God does not lie. If He said it, it is settled. Even in the midst of what looks like impossibility and what looks like a, no, even when all of the conditions say this thing really isn't going to happen, if God said it, believe it. We have to continually remind ourselves that we will not get discouraged, that we will not give up so that we do not go searching for God, leaving the very place that He is. On this journey called life, we have to continually remind ourselves that we really believe God.

REFRESHING KEY #45
On this journey called life, you must continually remind yourself that you really believe God!

When you are on a quest to discover your peace and make sense of what is going on around you, you cannot be weighted down with frustration and anger. As soon as you step outside of the boat and attempt to walk on the water you will find yourself sinking because of the frustration and the anger that you are carrying. However, when you tap into your faith in God and give your burdens to Him, your load is lightened, you discover your inner peace and you become acquainted with the calm. At that point you are discovering the peace of God that is living on the inside of you, the peace of God that passes all understanding, the peace of God that allows you to be in the midst of a storm but not panic. You can look around in the midst of chaos and see God.

"And the peace of God, which passeth all understanding, shall keep your hearts and minds through Christ Jesus."
(Philippians 4:7)

Let go of whatever causes you to be earthbound - worry, fear, disappointment. Stop trying to solve issues that only God can solve. When you try to solve problems that only God can solve you are earthbound. You take your eyes off of the Spirit realm and you focus on the problems of this natural world.

Our ultimate assignment on the earth is to complete the assignment that Father sent each of us here to complete. Regardless of your individual giftings, we were all sent here for a purpose. If we fail to tap into our purpose or tap into purpose today, worry tomorrow and fear the next, we stay in a perpetual motion of starting and stopping, always having to start over from the beginning. But if you realize that you are here for a reason, you are not here by happenstance, you are not here by chance, you are not just here because your mother and father decided to get together, but God dropped you in the earth for a purpose, then you can begin to tackle life victoriously.

You have to let go of the baggage. You have to let go of the things that will keep you earthbound and allow yourself to be free to soar, to take flight and to do the thing that God has destined you to do.

"Hast thou not known? hast thou not heard, that the everlasting God, the LORD, the Creator of the ends of the earth, fainteth not, neither is weary? There is no searching of his understanding. He giveth power to the faint; and to them that have no might he increaseth strength. Even the youths shall faint and be weary, and the young men shall utterly fall: But they that wait upon the LORD shall renew their strength; they shall mount up with wings as eagles; they shall run, and not be weary; and they shall walk, and not faint." (Isaiah 40:28-31)

You have to be like the eagle that is able to fly high above the clouds. You cannot fly if you are worried about "stuff." But when you allow yourself to let God take care of your needs and you concentrate on fulfilling the assignment that He has given to you, then He will allow you to soar. Allow yourself to drop the baggage and the dead weight of others and take flight. Allow nothing or no one to hold you back, because the very breath of God is your strength.

In every season of our lives God knows what we need. Once we begin to cast our cares on Him, when we understand that this is a great way of discovering the peace of God and discovering who God is we will realize that this peace that we have is contagious. It will affect the lives of those around us. The Spirit of God will move not just on our behalf, but on the behalf of those who are in our environment, those who might be in the same room, in the same class, on the same job.

When Paul and Silas prayed, the prison doors opened and things began to shake around them. However, when the prison doors opened they did not experience the breakthrough by themselves. Every prisoner experienced the breakthrough, every prisoner experienced the peace, every prisoner experienced the joy and elation.

REFRESHING KEY #46
Drop the dead weight and allow yourself to fly!

Once you get ahold of the peace of God, the peace that passes all understanding, you are able to be of good cheer because you have rested in your belief. You can hear God echoing things in your ear. You can see God moving in your life. You have begun the process of self-discovery. When you no longer find yourself sinking and drowning in the worries that used to bother you, when you find yourself moving past the foolishness around you, then you know that you are discovering a new part of your life.

"Now it is God who makes both us and you stand firm in Christ. He anointed us, set his seal of ownership on us, and put his Spirit in our hearts as a deposit, guaranteeing what is to come."
(2 Corinthians 1:21-22)

Chapter Eight
MOVE!

"Faith is taking the first step even when you don't see the whole staircase." ~Dr. Martin Luther King, Jr.

Don't Just Sit There... Do Something!

"And there were four leprous men at the entering in of the gate: and they said one to another, Why sit we here until we die? If we say, We will enter into the city, then the famine is in the city, and we shall die there: and if we sit still here, we die also."
(2 Kings 7:3-4)

The antidote for worry is working on purpose. You can move beyond your worry about things that are happening in your natural, if you can put your mind on the assignment that the Father has given you. It can appear to the natural eye that things are falling apart around you, but the best way to take your focus off of what is happening around you is to put your focus on what God is doing through you. Let's face it, whether you look at your situation or not, it is going to be what it is going to be until God decides to change it.

So, why sit there and watch things unravel? When you watch them unravel, when you watch things break down, you may start to assess what is happening incorrectly. You may try to patch things up when God is saying to let it go, or you may try to patch it up in your own way, putting things here, putting things there, trying to plug the holes, when God is saying I am working on something new.

REFRESHING KEY #47
God is doing a new thing!

Why sit there and watch things unravel? You can take your mind off your natural experience when you are in a place of peace. You can take your mind off of it when you work on purpose, when you do the assignment that God has called you to do, the thing that will bless other people. While God is working out your situation, keep your mind focused on what He is asking you to do, on your God-given assignment, on your piece of the puzzle.

The scripture says you will have a peace that passes all understanding. That means it will not make sense to the human mind. It will cause the human mind to say, how can you continue to do this when you know that this is happening? But when your mind is fixed on purpose, when you really trust God, when you really do like the scripture says and believe God, then you purpose in your heart to do what God created you to do because He said so. Refuse to sit idly and watch things unravel. Refuse to focus on the seemingly insurmountable problem. Take your eyes off of it, because the One who has everything under control, our Father, is already taking care of everything. You have to be convinced in your heart that you really trust Him, and you have to be convinced in your mind that you truly believe God.

You have to get to a point where you are no longer allowing the spirit of selfishness to creep into your life. Now is not the time for you to have a pity party. Realize that if you are in a situation, there is a purpose for it. It may seem dark, it may appear as if you are losing, but God has a plan. He is working it all together for your good. There is a purpose for it.

"To every thing there is a season, and a time to every purpose under the heaven." (Ecclesiastes 3:1)

God wants to use you so that others can benefit from seeing your peace. Others will want to be around you when they see that you are keeping your eyes on God. I can imagine what went through some of those prisoners' minds as they heard Paul and Silas pray and they began to witness the outpouring of God's promise and His love. God does not send trials in our lives for no reason. There is always a reason. There is always a purpose God will always use man to show forth His glory. If you can rest in the peace of God, if you can keep your eyes focused on God while you are going through a storm, others will watch you and learn how to exercise faith instead of fear, peace instead of panic, strength instead of weakness.

They too will not allow the issues of this world to overtake them, overwhelm them, disappoint them or render them out of the fight. They will realize that they can go through the vicissitudes of life and not give up. They can have the victory in the battle. Not only did God have a purpose for all of the great saints of old, but he has a purpose for your life. You are not here by accident or by happenstance, but you are here because the Father still has a plan for your life.

"An individual has not started living until he can rise above the narrow confines of his individualistic concerns to the broader concerns of all humanity." (Martin Luther King, Jr.)

Completing the Work

God has a plan for your life. Oftentimes when people hear that God has a plan for their lives or when Christians profess to others that God has a plan for their lives, oftentimes they say it without really thinking about the magnitude of that blessing. God has a plan. It is really a well thought out plan. It is a delicately carved out plan. It is an assignment.

On your natural job, the company has plans for you being there. They have a particular assignment for you to accomplish. Faithful workers will show up every day, rain, shine, sick, tired, it doesn't matter, because they know that the employer has an assignment for them to complete. They will do it because they know at the end there is a reward, some type of monetary compensation that will allow them to live. Many people do it because they have to do it. Some people are blessed to be able to do the thing that they were created to do, so they enjoy doing it.

REFRESHING KEY #48
Do it in excellence, with excellence and for Excellence!

We must have the same commitment to our kingdom assignment, the assignment that was divinely given to us by our Heavenly Father. When we think about God's plan for lives, our God-given assignment, we have to look at it in the same way as the secular job. If God told me to do it, I am not going to cancel it. I am not going to ignore it. I am not going to put some other things before it. I am not going to keep putting it on the back burner nor put it off till tomorrow. I am not going to do it haphazardly, halfheartedly or sporadically. I am going to do it in excellence, with excellence and for Excellence.

The same principles that you apply to succeed on your natural job you must exercise in your kingdom assignment, for the reward is greater. On your natural job you receive a paycheck. On your kingdom assignment you receive eternal life. You receive a greater reward. More importantly, God is the source of your natural job and your kingdom assignment and He is the ultimate controller of everything that concerns you. Just as you seek the approval of your natural employer, you must seek the approval of the Father, the CEO of your life, so that in the end you can say, *"Father, I have completed the assignment you have given me,"* and you can hear your Father say, *"Well done thy good and faithful servant."*

We can be still in the midst of a storm. In the midst of people being disgruntled, losing hope and losing sight of God, what a powerful testimony it is to know that we can be in the midst of all of that, yet be still and know that the victory is ours. In the midst of panic and devastation, you can be still and know that your God, your Father has everything under control.

Letting Go

"The Lord is my shepherd I shall not want. He makes me to lie down in green pastures. He restores my soul. He leads me beside the still waters." (Psalm 23:1-2)

127

Stress is very dangerous to the physical body. It affects the mind and body. Heart disease, diabetes, headaches, cancer can all result from high levels of stress and worry. Do not worry about the things of which you have no control. Sometimes you have to let go of the wheel and let God drive. Stop trying to patch it up. Stop trying to work it out and just let God do it. That is the place of peace. You can rest because you know that God is your source. If the Lord is your shepherd, then you can go through this life worry-free. You can be courageous and live in peace. The Father desires for us to remain in a state of peace.

REFRESHING KEY #49
The Source has always been God!

You have to throw your hands up in worship. In the midst of it all, choose to worship. In the midst of it all, choose to be at peace. Regardless of how it looks, rest and know who has everything under control. You have to say, *"the Lord is my shepherd, I shall not want."* You have to keep tapping into the source. There is only one source and that is God. Man can pretend to be your source, but God uses whomever He chooses to give you the provision that you need in a particular season. The Source is God. The Source has always been God. The source has never been Man.

When a car is spinning out of control you are told to let go of the wheel, because eventually it will straighten itself up. That is how life is. When life is spinning out of control, you have to let go. Stop fighting. Just let it go so that you can discover the peace of God. Let go so that those who are watching your life spin out of control can glean from it. Let go so that people can look at your life and know that the only reason you are where you are now, the only way you could have come out of that situation is by the mighty hand of God.

Let go of the wheel so that you can walk into the understanding of who God is in your life. You may be busy, but you will have a breakthrough. You may be tired, but you will have victory, because you will understand and prove to others that there is only one God and He has everything under control. All you have to do is let go of the wheel.

REFRESHING KEY #50
Stop trying to fix it. Let God work a miracle!

When you let go, you allow God to work a miracle. Stop trying to hold on. Stop trying to fix it. Stop worrying about it every day. Today it feels right and tomorrow it doesn't, one moment it is right and the next minute it falls apart. That is a clear indication that God is trying to work a miracle and you may be running interference with the miracle.

Sometimes I think Father is saying, *"If you can just take your hands off of it and allow me to work the miracle, I can deliver you quickly."* When you try to fix something for your children and they keep putting their hands in it, you say, "just give me one minute, I am trying to fix it for you," but they continue to help. Sometimes we try to interfere with God working a miracle. When you are at the place where things do not seem like they are falling in line, no matter what you do it seems like the situation stays the same or gets perpetually worse, that is a good indication that God is trying to work a miracle.

When you have done all that you can do to stand, you have to stand therefore. (Ephesians 6:13). When you have done everything that you can do and it still does not rectify the situation, it is a sign that God is knocking at your door with a miracle. The woman with the issue of blood tried to work out her own situation for 38 years. However, when she came to herself, became still and heard the instruction of God within herself she was healed immediately - MIRCALE!

There are many who are walking in that revelation right now. There are those who are reading this book right now who know that the Father is up to something in their lives. You can't explain it, but you continue to seek God. There is something about the peace of God that will change your life. If you should ever fully embrace His peace, you will wake up every morning with a smile on your face regardless of what is happening in your natural experience.

REFRESHING KEY #51
God himself is moving and creating some great things on your behalf!

Sometimes you have to have an "I don't care" attitude. It doesn't matter what is happening, the peace of God will prevail. I don't care what the situation looks like, the peace of God will prevail. God is continually giving us signs to let us know that everything is going to be all right. God himself is moving and creating some great things on our behalf. All you have to do is put your trust in the Father, lean on him and know that He has everything under control.

Many have allowed people to convince them that the negative feelings that they have are normal and that they should embrace them. But we are not called to embrace them. We are called to get rid of them. We are commanded to cast our cares on Him, learn from them, grow from them, become better because of them. There are many people holding on to negative feelings from 30 years ago, 40 years ago, two hours ago, a minute ago, and if they do not begin to release them, the negativity will weigh them down, stunt their growth and render them out of the race of life.

We are not designed to hold on to negativity. We are designed to let it go. We are designed to hold on to the creative power that God has given us. We are called to hold on to the mind of Christ that God has given us. He called us to hold on to peace and love and everything that is good for mankind. Those things that are not good for us that are toxic to our bodies and to our minds and to our health, we are called to get rid of it. If we don't get rid of it, it will destroy us.

There is a reason why God continually commands us in scripture to be at peace, to not get weary in our well doing, to not worry, to be of good courage and of good cheer. God knows all of the hurdles that we are going to have to leap over in this life. He knows all of the challenges that we are going to face. He knows the different pitfalls into which we may run. But Father never wants us to get off of our assignment. He believes in His creation. If we keep our eyes focused on Him, we will not get off course. The Father needs for us to fulfill our assignment, regardless of what his happening in our natural lives.

REFRESHING KEY #52
God's reward is great!

He created us to be able to fulfill His assignment in the earth. That is very critical. God created you because He needed to get something done in the universe through you. Yes, you are going to have to go through different challenges, but know that you are going to be able to overcome them. The more hurdles you can leap and the more obstacles you can overcome, will determine the number of people you will be able to bring into His presence and make His name known in a greater way. His reward is great.

"But without faith it is impossible to please him: for he that cometh to God must believe that he is, and that he is a rewarder of them that diligently seek him." (Hebrews 11:6)

People are searching. Regardless of where they are situated in the universe, regardless of their geographic location, everyone seeks to understand why God placed them in the earth. From the multibillionaire, to the person who is living on very meager means, everyone wants to know their purpose, everyone wants to know who they really are and they are not satisfied until they have discovered it. When your mind is enlightened, when the light bulb comes on that you are here for God not for yourself, that he really sent you here for a purpose, you will be fulfilled and others will be blessed.

Be Grateful

"In every thing give thanks: for this is the will of God in Christ Jesus concerning you." (1 Thessalonians 5:18)

No matter what is happening in your life, be grateful. Don't complain about what you see in your natural experience that you do not like. Manifest what God has placed in you to manifest. But in everything, through the trials, through the storms, through the ups and through the downs, thank God for the gift of life and the opportunity to wake up each day fresh and attempt to get it right. When you understand your purpose and God's plan for your life, worry is not an option. Peace is the agenda for the day. However, you cannot get that kind of peace by accident.

REFRESHING KEY #53
Be grateful on purpose!

You do not develop a heart of gratitude by accident. It is purpose-driven. Something on the inside of you pushes you and allows you to express the truth of who God is in your life. It is not by happenstance. It does not just fall out of the sky. You do not wake up one morning and see everything that the Father promised to you manifest. Only those who are purposefully grateful, purposefully thankful and consciously aware of God 24/7 will receive the fullness of what God has for their lives.

The more you focus on purpose, the more you realize the things that you need to add to your life and the things that you need to subtract from my life. There are some things that you should keep carrying through this life and there are some things you need to dump.

Paul and Silas prayed and the atmosphere shifted. You cannot create that type of environment by accident. The walls did not come down by accident. David did not kill Goliath by accident. Moses did not tell Pharaoh to let the people go by accident. It was all about purpose. When you understand your purpose and you understand that the very things that are happening to you are not by accident, but they are designed and created by the Father so that He can get the very best out of you, you will no longer complain. You will be thankful. You will not be angry. You will be grateful. You will realize that your life is bigger than an argument, bigger than a disagreement. Your life is bigger than any negative event that is happening to you.

Once you tap into purpose and realize that nothing happens in your life by accident, that you must seek the higher mind of God and the higher revelation of God, your life will be better immediately. You will immediately be made whole. It is all about perspective. If you do not understand the purpose of your life, abuse is inevitable.

REFRESHING KEY #54
If you do not understand the purpose of your life, abuse is inevitable!

You have to know that God has created you to do something and then you have to do that thing on purpose. If you decide to stay at a place of unforgiveness, a place of worry, a place of discontentment, dissatisfaction, then you know that you are not focused on purpose. You are idle. Be about doing the Father's business. Jesus was focused on fulfilling His assignment. *"And he said unto them, How is it that ye sought me? wist ye not that I must be about my Father's business?"* (Luke 2:49)

Those of us who know what it feels like to carry the plan of God, to birth the purpose of God in the earth, those of us who knows what it feels like to carry the weight of His glory know that regardless of what is happening in your natural world you must keep pushing toward purpose. The glory of the Lord is weighty because you have to look past so many things in the natural and keep moving toward Spirit. If you find that you are ready to give up and you allow the cares of the world to overwhelm you, stop, take a breath and remember what the Father has assigned you to do.

When you really are about your assignment and purpose, when you know you are trying to birth something huge, you cannot allow your energy to be focused on the small stuff. You cannot sweat the small stuff. It is impossible to sweat the small stuff and still get the big stuff accomplished. You can't sweat small stuff and birth purpose and greatness. It is impossible. It depletes your energy. All of the good energy that you should be putting behind your assignment, you put behind worry, struggle, arguments and a continual state of feeling overwhelmed.

David said, *"When my heart is overwhelmed lead me to the rock that's higher than I."* (Psalm 61:2) Lead me to something greater. Elevate me. The Father will lead you to the rock that is higher than you, higher than your circumstance, higher than your situation, higher than whatever you are dealing with in the natural. When you are not overwhelmed you can wake up every day excited about purpose. If your home is being foreclosed on, you are still excited, because God has led you to the rock that is higher. Your finances may be low, but you are still excited, because He has led you to the rock that is higher. You may have lost your job,

135

but you are still excited, because the Father has led you to the rock that is higher and has allowed you to gain a greater perspective about what He is doing in your life.

REFRESHING KEY #55
Don't allow distractions to throw you off course!

There is no need to stay in a state of feeling overwhelmed, there is no productivity there. You do not want negativity to multiply. You can get a chain of negativity going quicker than a chain of testimonies about the greatness of God. A negative report travels faster than a positive report. When your heart is overwhelmed the Father will lead you to the rock that is higher and He allows your mind to be focused on completing your assignment.

Don't allow distractions to throw you off course. By the time you rest from focusing on the small stuff you won't have any energy left. Just let go of the wheel and let God drive. Paul and Silas had no idea what the outcome was going to be when they prayed and they sang. They had no idea the miracle that they were generating. They had no idea of the power that they possessed at that moment.

Once you understand the power that you possess, you too can cause the very grounds to shake around you. You too can cause those around you to live at a higher level in God. We can cause those around us to look and see that God is still doing some great things in the earth when we are moving on purpose, when we are allowing the peace of God that passes all understanding to speak louder than the negativity in our lives.

Move in that understanding. Allow your life to be elevated to a higher level of thought in God. Then you will know that you are moving in purpose. Walk on top of your situations and do not allow yourself to be pulled down by them. Remember what God has told you and believe Him for it. Then you will know that you are whole.

"Wherefore, sirs, be of good cheer: for I believe God, that it shall be even as it was told me." (Acts 27:25)

Chapter Nine
POSITIONED TO WIN!

"For I know the plans I have for you," declares the Lord,
"plans to prosper you and not to harm you, plans to give you hope
and a future." (Jeremiah 29:11)

Taking Care of Business

Steven was very co-dependent. He always depended on someone else to take care of the things he should have been able to take care of for himself. Steven was 40 years-old and had not held a steady job in 10 years. At age 30, Steven worked as a production assistant at a radio station. He loved his job and had dreams of owning his own radio station in the future.

But Steven hit a bump in the road. The radio station he worked for was unexpectedly shut down and Steven found himself unemployed. He was devastated by the news and Steven lost his fervor for his passion. He tried to find other positions, but the doors were always shut in his face. Steven was unable to find another position in radio. He became very discouraged and demotivated.

At the age of 40, Steven was at a standstill. He lived with his mother, then with his sister, then with a friend and now was dependent upon a girlfriend to take care of him. In Steven's view, someone had to always take care of him, because he was not motivated to take care of himself.

One night Steven had a dream that he owned a radio station. His dream was so vivid it felt like it was real. He saw the players involved. He saw his radio station blessing the people in his community. Steven awakened from his sleep and was convicted. He was puzzled why he let one stumbling block in his life stop him from moving forward in his dream. He longed for his independence. He longed to be free in his mind to pursue his dreams. He longed for change.

"Before I formed you in the womb I knew you, before you were born I set you apart..." (Jeremiah 1:5)

Steven's mother felt his pain. One day she called and asked him to go to church with her. She knew that if she could introduce Steven to her God, the Creator, then the Creator would tell the "creation" how to function. Steven's mother knew that his connection with God was the key to his pursuit of purpose. Steven felt he was at the end of his rope, so he decided to be obedient to his mother's advice and accept her invitation. That evening they went to church and for the first time Steven heard the voice of God for himself.

For the first time in 10 years Steven's spirit was awakened. He felt motivated. He felt excited about life. Steven left that service and went on an active pursuit of his purpose. He began to ask questions of God and God began to give him answers. Steven began to get his swagger back. He woke up every morning bright and early with the intention to find a job. He knew that was the first hurdle he had to leap. Less than one week later, Steven was offered a job at Wal-Mart stocking shelves, but he continued to pursue his passion. Steven's life was changing right before his very eyes.

PURPOSE + PASSION = HIS DIVINE PLAN!

Steven was a new person. His life was opening up for the good. Over the next six months, Steven submitted his resume to many radio stations, and after a year he landed his dream job at one of the top radio stations. He saw God's favor in action and he also saw the power of believing in his dream, believing in himself and believing in His God. Steven's life was rejuvenated. His obedience to the voice of God radically changed his thought process and ultimately, his life.

Today, Steven is writing his business plan to purchase a radio station and gathering all that he will need in the natural to make his dream a reality. He is preparing his mind for where he is going, knowing that his obedience is better than sacrifice.

It's so amazing to wake up in the morning knowing that the Father still has some things for you to do and that He is still using you to reflect His Glory and Awesomeness in the Earth. There is nothing like being PURPOSE-DRIVEN, fulfilling the assignment that God has placed you in the earth to fulfill. Stay in expectation, because there are blessings attached to your obedience.

Get Into Position

"I'm not saying that I have this all together, that I have it made. But I am well on my way, reaching out for Christ, who has so wondrously reached out for me. Friends, don't get me wrong: By

no means do I count myself an expert in all of this, but I've got my eye on the goal, where God is beckoning us onward—to Jesus. I'm off and running, and I'm not turning back. So let's keep focused on that goal, those of us who want everything God has for us. If any of you have something else in mind, something less than total commitment, God will clear your blurred vision—you'll see it yet! Now that we're on the right track, let's stay on it. Stick with me, friends. Keep track of those you see running this same course, headed for this same goal. There are many out there taking other paths, choosing other goals, and trying to get you to go along with them. I've warned you of them many times; sadly, I'm having to do it again. All they want is easy street. They hate Christ's Cross. But easy street is a dead-end street. Those who live there make their bellies their gods; belches are their praise; all they can think of is their appetites." (Philippians 3:12-19 - Message Bible)

We must reflect on the greatness that God has placed on the inside of us so that we can position ourselves to win in this life. Paul said I am reaching for Christ. I know I don't have it all together and that I have made mistakes, but it is through prayer that I get my answers from God. It is through prayer that I win this race. It is prayer that can shift and change the foundation of this world, if we can just pray with a pure heart and a pure mind and pray according to God's agenda for our lives, God's plan. When we operate according to God's agenda we can do like Paul, run forward with a determination of not turning back.

Repeat the following affirmation with me for 30 days. Repeat it every morning when you first wake up and every evening before you go to sleep. Then write it 100 times, three times day, for the next 30 days.

*"I am not turning back. This time I am on course.
I am allowing God to position me to win!"*

Keep God's vision for you in focus and decide that you are not going to turn back. And when you get weary and it feels like the weight of the world is on your shoulders, when it feels like the pressures of life are going to overtake you and you feel like you are losing your breath, run to someone who you know can get a prayer through and will pray with your divine destiny in mind. Everyone cannot pray for you. You have to get those who can see in the Spirit the course that God has set for your life.

Your prayer must be focused. It can be as long as you want it to be or as short as you want it to be, but it must be a focused prayer. Oftentimes people pray for things that do not fit in God's plan for their life. We have to pray God's "expected end," the end that is going to allow us to win, the end that along the journey is going to bless others and fulfill the ultimate plan of God for our lives. You must stay on course for the journey no matter what comes your way. In this season, it is critical that you position yourself to win.

Prayer - The Key Position

"...men ought always to pray, and not to faint." (Luke 18:1)

Prayer plays a vital role in positioning ourselves to win this race. It is impossible to have the victories and accomplishments that we are trying to receive from God if our life is not devoted to Him in prayer. Without prayer we will fall short, because we will not be able to hear God whisper in our ear in the midst of the chaos that is happening around us.

The Bible says, *"Men ought to always pray and not faint."* We should always be in His presence. We should seek is face 24 hours a day, seven days a week. It is such a critical point to remain in a posture of prayer. It is one of the positions to win. Without God we can do nothing.

No need to try to figure out all of these situations that happen on this earthly realm, try to fight the struggles and the battles on your own when we have the divine answer resting on the inside of us, when we have God who will continually speak to us. If we just quiet ourselves and position ourselves to hear him, He will give us the strategies that we need in order to endure so that we can attain the prize at the end. You should be bringing everything that is of concern to God in prayer. You should be saying to God, *"Father, I've tried all I can do. Now, I am falling at your mercy seat. Help me to understand the things I don't understand."*

It is through prayer that we tap into the mind of God. It is through prayer that we receive divine instructions from God to move forward and to become all that we were destined to become in this life.

REFRESHING KEY #56
Proper prayer eliminates our doubt and our fears!

Proper prayer eliminates our doubt and our fears. The Bible says that a double-minded man is unstable in all of his ways

(James 1:8). Many people do not have a problem praying. They have a problem believing that God will answer their prayers. It is easy to become overwhelmed by worldly circumstances. Even the strongest believers grapple with unbelief at some points in their lives. We cannot go before God and pray for victory, breakthroughs and miracles and as soon as we stop praying begin to fear that what we have prayed for will not come to pass. We must stand and believe God will answer that which we have already prayed.

Prayer gives us the strength to trust God and believe him at his word. Therefore, it is critical that we stay in the posture of prayer. When we stay in the posture of prayer we do not allow any room for doubt and fear to step in and destabilize us. This is critical in a season where so many things can come to overwhelm us and cause us to live in fear and doubt. But when we understand that God has already designed for us to win, all we need to do is listen to his voice and allow ourselves to be positioned in the right place.

The Importance of Positioning

"Do you not know that in a race all the runners run, but only one gets the prize? Run in such a way as to get the prize."
(1 Corinthians 9:24)

If you break a bone in your arm, in order for it to heal, the doctor must set the bone in the correct position. If you break a bone in your arm, in order to cure the issue, you need to have the bone set it in the right position. If it is not set it in the correct position, then it will be out of alignment and will cause you

145

problems and pain in the future. Even if it is set just slightly off, you will find that you won't be able to move as fluently as you were once able to move.

That is the way it is with God. You have to be able to allow God to position you in the right place. You can feel like you have positioned yourself in the right place, but if you do not allow God to do the positioning, you will wake up one day and realize that you are out of alignment.

We can be fooled into believe that because everything is going well we do not need to pray. But you may not have been the one to pray for where you are and what you have received. There was a grandmother, a great grandmother, a grandfather in your lineage that prayed for you and now the word of Lord and the favor of God are manifesting in your life, not because of what you did not do, not because of the way you think, but because of what someone did for you.

REFRESHING KEY #57
Get into position!

Many of us are reaping the benefits of a praying mother, a praying grandmother or praying great grandparents who prayed that our situation would be so much different than theirs, that our lives would be so much greater than what they experienced at that time, who saw prophetically who God created you to be. Although you may have had some twists and turns in your life, if you remain focused on God and believe who God created you to be, the positive results of their prayers will manifest in your life. That is the power of prayer, one of the first and foremost positions to winning in this life. It reaches through generations.

Live... Pursue... Plan

"So shall my word be that goeth forth out of my mouth: it shall not return unto me void, but it shall accomplish that which I please, and it shall prosper in the thing whereto I sent it."
(Isaiah 55:11)

Prayer lasts. Prayer changes things. Prayer changes you. It may not change the things in your natural surroundings that you can see right at the moment, but in the Spirit, God has already sent an answer. Do not be fooled in this hour. Do not think for a moment that you can win without prayer. We cannot look at the situations in the world or the situations in our own environment and say that prayer does not work. There are many people who are ready to give up right now because they prayed for something a month ago, a week ago, a year ago, and they are not seeing the results of their prayers. They feel as if they have gone before God and asked God to do something on their behalf and God didn't hear them. If you want win, you must pursue God, follow His plan and live according to his purpose for your life.

I want to encourage you to keep praying. Keep trusting in your God and know that God will answer your prayers. He may not answer you in the time and the season that you want him to answer, but keep praying, keep believing, because the word of God cannot come back to him void. If it came back void, God would be a liar. Our God is not a man that he should lie. Don't try to manipulate God to work in your timeframe. You must believe in your heart and not doubt that you will see the thing that you have prayed for come to pass in your life. You will see the prophecy that has been spoken over your life come to pass, and you will know only God did it. It takes a real champion who trusts God to position himself to win.

REFRESHING KEY #58
In the pressing, He is realigning you!

We have to press through the adverse, the contrary and the negative and allow God to position us according to His plan. In that pressing he is realigning us, because somewhere along the journey we may have gotten a little off course from His original intent for our lives. If you believe that what God said is true, then you will align yourself with the purpose and plan that God has for your life. If you believe that God has placed greatness, purpose and destiny inside of you (which He has), then regardless of the obstacles, pitfalls and the situations that come your way, he will remember you at the appointed time and the appointed season. Not only that, God has a plan for your children's lives. You have to position yourself to win for them while they are yet beginning to understand what God is saying for their lives.

Position yourself to win today, not tomorrow, not five years from now - TODAY! You have already won, regardless of what you have to face five minutes from now, two hours from now, twenty-five days from now. The bottom line is you have already won. Allow yourself to go through the process of life, because what you see in your natural is temporary, but what God has for you in Spirit is eternal.

Focus on the eternal plan of God for your life, those eternal benefits that last, that can withstand any challenge. If we keep our position to win and stay in the posture of prayer, we will be able to withstand anything.

Affirm...

"I now position myself to win. I now receive divine instructions from God. All things are answered for me. I open myself to receive and hear what God is saying to me in this hour."

Are you pursuing your passion?

Are you pursuing your purpose?

Are you doing the thing that the Father placed you in the Earth to do?

Nothing happens by accident! God sent you here for a specific reason. You must be determined to fulfill the plan that the Father intended for you. How do you do this? You have to <u>live</u> on PURPOSE, <u>pursue</u> your PASSION and <u>manifest</u> the PLAN, for therein lies the wellspring of blessings for someone else's life. **LIVE...PURSUE...PLAN!** That's right! Your obedience to God is directly connected to the miracles that are earmarked for someone else's life!

"And these signs will accompany those who believe..."
(Mark 16:17)

From the Desk of Pastor Je'Nise Goss

My Friends, meditate on the ***Refreshing Thoughts and Affirmations*** that God is speaking.
Allow them to solidify in your spirit and help position you to win.
Time out for church as usual. We have to position ourselves to win in this life!

Father, we bless your name for this great day, another opportunity for your people to get it right, another opportunity to win today and stand in victory, regardless of the situations that are going on around us. As long as we remain in you, we can position ourselves to win.

I pray that today, once and for all, you will be able to shut down the noise that may be around you, whatever you're thinking about, whatever you're worrying about and bask in the presence of the Lord. Put your cares on the back burner.
I want you to hear the mind of God for you, knowing that the Father is taking care of your every need...

Thank you, Father, for your Refreshing Waters!

~Pastor Je'Nise Goss

REFRESHING AFFIRMATION #1

Far too often people allow their day to be dictated by others. Negative words, fear, misunderstandings, worry, sadness and doubt are the culprits to turning a great day (a day that the Lord has made) into a somber, miserable and dreadful day. Don't let your outward circumstances dictate your level of inner peace, joy and excitement. Don't let worry overshadow your GOD-expectation. If God said it, then He is will do it, regardless of what it looks like in your present circumstance.

REFRESHING AFFIRMATION #2

I am excited about what God is doing! Let that be your affirmation today... not only your affirmation, but believe it in your heart. Allow the promises of God to be the catalyst for your excitement and joy! *"For all the promises of God in him are yea, and in him Amen, unto the glory of God by us."*
(2 Corinthians 1:20)

REFRESHING AFFIRMATION #3

Isn't it awesome to know that the breath of God is within you? It means that all the good that God is, is living inside of you. Say with me, *"I want to reflect the works of my Father, the One who created me with purpose!"* Today, focus on reflecting the Christ that lives on the inside of you. Be the blessing to someone else. Speak words of life to someone else. Reflect the glory of God in every situation. Let your affirmation today be, *"All the good that God is lives on the inside of me!"*

~~~~~~~~~~~~~~~~~~~~~~~~~~~~~~~

REFRESHING AFFIRMATION #4

Today is NEW DAY!

~~~~~~~~~~~~~~~~~~~~~~~~~~~~~~~

REFRESHING AFFIRMATION #5

This is the day the Lord has made! Rejoice! Be thankful! Be grateful to the Father just because He is! Don't think about what you don't have. Dwell on and be thankful for all that you do have. Our God is awesome. Everything that He does, He does it well! I am thankful for the breath that He has given me today! Focus not on things, but focus on the eternal greatness of God and His unfailing, unconditional love for all of us, which is eternal and everlasting! His favor is amazing. His love is supreme. His plan and destiny for each and every one of us is breathtaking. We owe Him our eternal thanks. Let your affirmation today be, *"Lord, I thank you just for who you are!"*

~~~~~~~~~~~~~~~~~~~~~~~~~~~~~~~

REFRESHING AFFIRMATION #6

I am excited to be breathing the Father's air and grateful to be resting in His Presence! My heart is full with thanksgiving and gratefulness to God, the Master of the Universe, just because He is! He is just that good! Today, I continually retreat to that quiet place within, the place where God dwells, and tell Him thank you for living on the inside of me.

I am eternally grateful!

~~~~~~~~~~~~~~~~~~~~~~~~~~~~

REFRESHING AFFIRMATION #7

Listen closely to hear the Father's voice in this season.

~~~~~~~~~~~~~~~~~~~~~~~~~~~~

REFRESHING AFFIRMATION #8

Yes! Alive, breathing and living! Thank you, Lord!

~~~~~~~~~~~~~~~~~~~~~~~~~~~~

REFRESHING AFFIRMATION #9

The Lord is my shepherd. Therefore, I have everything that I need.

~~~~~~~~~~~~~~~~~~~~~~~~~~~~

REFRESHING AFFIRMATION #10
IT'S ALL GOD!

~~~~~~~~~~~~~~~~~~~~~~~~~~~~

REFRESHING AFFIRMATION #11

Today, don't allow negativity to linger in your atmosphere! Today is a day of focus! Focus on what God has assigned for you to do in this season. Focus on the promises of God that He made to you. Focus on that which the Father placed you in the earth to do. Focus on the Father's unconditional, unfailing love for you. As you focus on Him, think on Him, put your attention on Him (just because HE IS). You will truly see that he is working everything together (good and bad) for your good and for His glory! Take your eyes off of what is not going right and put attention on the good that is God and He will reveal to you the answers that you have been seeking! Proclaim within yourself, "I am God-Focused!"

"Finally, brethren, whatsoever things are true, whatsoever things are honest, whatsoever things are just, whatsoever things are pure, whatsoever things are lovely, whatsoever things are of good report; if there be any virtue, and if there be any praise, think on these things." (Philippians 4:8)

~~~~~~~~~~~~~~~~~~~~~~~~~~~~~

REFRESHING AFFIRMATION #12

If you are going through a challenging season or moment in time, remember... God is able! Whatever you do, don't doubt God's ability to deliver you. Be patient and wait on Him. There is nothing like God's timing. He does all things (I don't care what it is) well! Change is surely coming!

~~~~~~~~~~~~~~~~~~~~~~~~~~~~~

REFRESHING AFFIRMATION #13

I've got a feeling that everything is going to be all right.
Restoration has finally come.
You shall be satisfied!

"And the floors shall be full of wheat, and the vats shall overflow with wine and oil. And I will restore to you the years that the locust hath eaten, the cankerworm, and the caterpillar, and the palmerworm, my great army which I sent among you. And ye shall eat in plenty, and be satisfied, and praise the name of the Lord

your God, that hath dealt wondrously with you: and my people shall never be ashamed." (Joel 2:24-26)

~~~~~~~~~~~~~~~~~~~~~~~~~~

REFRESHING AFFIRMATION #14

God is not man. God is God. If He promised it, He will bring it to pass. If He said it, He will do it. Put your trust in God and let it stay there. The question is not will God manifest his promise in your life. The question is can you believe God and not doubt? I don't care what it looks like in your natural... You must choose to believe God! Whose report are you going to believe?

"God is not a man, that he should lie, nor a son of man, that he should change his mind. Does he speak and then not act? Does he promise and not fulfill?" (Numbers 23:19)

~~~~~~~~~~~~~~~~~~~~~~~~~~

REFRESHING AFFIRMATION #15

This is the air I breathe... Be Grateful!

~~~~~~~~~~~~~~~~~~~~~~~~~~

REFRESHING AFFIRMATION #16

Speak Lord, for your servant is listening!

~~~~~~~~~~~~~~~~~~~~~~~~~~

REFRESHING AFFIRMATION #17

I am absolutely beyond excited this morning for the opportunity to breathe! Thank you, Father! Great and mighty is our God! He alone is worthy! My focus is clear. I know who I am. I am overwhelmed by His love and His favor. Greatness lives on the inside of me!

REFRESHING AFFIRMATION #18

What is your divine affirmation this morning? Speak into the atmosphere!

REFRESHING AFFIRMATION #19

So grateful that the Father still has work for me to do!

REFRESHING AFFIRMATION #20

I'm standing on His promises!
"..for they that wait upon the Lord shall renew their strength; they shall mount up with wings as eagles; they shall run, and not be weary; and they shall walk, and not faint." (Isaiah 40:31)

REFRESHING AFFIRMATION #21

My Heavenly Father always keeps his promise. God always keeps His promise.

I am so glad that the Sovereign Lord has had and will always have everything in control! He has the whole world (100%) in his hands. In him do I trust!

~~~~~~~~~~~~~~~~~~~~~~~~~~~~~~

REFRESHING AFFIRMATION #22
Today, gratefulness is flowing from my heart. Overwhelmed by the Father's love. He is just that GOOD!

~~~~~~~~~~~~~~~~~~~~~~~~~~~~~~

REFRESHING AFFIRMATION #23
This is the day that the Lord has made and I am excited and happy glad! Thank you, Father!

~~~~~~~~~~~~~~~~~~~~~~~~~~~~~~

REFRESHING AFFIRMATION #24
Thankful, grateful and ready to manifest another piece of my divine assignment! Affirm within yourself, "Today, I am manifesting! No obstacles can stand in my way. No negative words, negative thoughts or negative people can hinder or stop what God has for me! My steps are ordered by my Father. I am in great expectation of Him, I trust Him, and I am excited about what God is doing in my life!" Now, shout... MANIFEST!

~~~~~~~~~~~~~~~~~~~~~~~~~~~~~~

REFRESHING AFFIRMATION #25
Today, I am watching His Divine favor unfold in my life.
It is absolutely, breathtaking and overwhelming. My God is
awesome!

~~~~~~~~~~~~~~~~~~~~~~~~~~~~~~

REFRESHING AFFIRMATION #26
If God said it, He will do it! That's my testimony!
I am seeing the manifestation of His word!
God is so good!

~~~~~~~~~~~~~~~~~~~~~~~~~~~~~~

REFRESHING AFFIRMATION #27
And God said, "Let there be! Speak your divine purpose and
destiny into existence! Speak what God has commanded you to
manifest in the earth! "If you are willing and obedient, you shall
eat the good of the land." (Isaiah 1:19) Speak into the atmosphere
that which God has commanded to manifest in your life and you
shall be satisfied!

~~~~~~~~~~~~~~~~~~~~~~~~~~~~~~

REFRESHING AFFIRMATION #28
Unlimited possibilities are revealed when you follow God's plan!
Walk In His Favor!

~~~~~~~~~~~~~~~~~~~~~~~~~~~~~~

REFRESHING AFFIRMATION #29

Today is a day of manifestation!
I can feel it in the air!
It is in the atmosphere!
If you know there are some things in you that must manifest, that must come to pass because God said so, shout, MANIFEST!
Keep your eyes open!
You don't want to miss the signs today that come to testify that He is manifesting His promises in your life!

~~~~~~~~~~~~~~~~~~~~~~~~~~~~~~~~

REFRESHING AFFIRMATION #30

"So if the Son liberates you [makes you free men], then you are really and unquestionably free." (John 8:36, AMP)

FREEDOM!

Thank you, Father, for the Freedom to pursue purpose… What a privilege! If you know you are FREE, then celebrate your FREEDOM and MANIFEST!

Affirm… I AM WALKING IN MY FREEDOM!

www.ingramcontent.com/pod-product-compliance
Lightning Source LLC
Chambersburg PA
CBHW051839090426
42736CB00011B/1889